My Darlings

My Darlings

A Memoir

By Grace Mather-Smith
Edited by her great-grandson
Russell P. Kelley, III

HAMILTON BOOKS
Lanham • Boulder • New York • London

The Rowman & Littlefield Publishing Group, Inc.
An imprint of The Rowman & Littlefield Publishing Group, Inc.
4501 Forbes Boulevard, Suite 200, Lanham, Maryland 20706
Hamilton Books Acquisitions Department (301) 459-3366

Unit A, Whitacre Mews, 26-34 Stannary Street, London SE11 4AB

British Library Cataloguing in Publication Information Available

Library of Congress Cataloging-in-Publication Data

Library of Congress Control Number: 2018959314
ISBN: 978-0-7618-7083-8 (paper)
ISBN: 978-0-7618-7084-5 (electronic)

∞™ The paper used in this publication meets the minimum requirements
of American National Standard for Information Sciences—Permanence
of Paper for Printed Library Materials, ANSI/NISO Z39.48-1992.

Printed in the United States of America

To Annie
from her grandnephew

Contents

List of Figures

Preface by the Editor

When I read my great-grandmother's memoir, I found myself alternately moved by her poetic descriptions of the Florida wilderness at the dawn of the twentieth century, and laughing out loud at her many hilarious anecdotes about her life in Denver, Chicago, Oakland (Florida) and beyond.

Grace Ruby Hamilton Smith Mather-Smith (which she trimmed to Grace Mather-Smith) finished her memoir in 1951, when she was 67 years old, and addressed it to her three children ("My Darlings"), who at that time all had families of their own. Grace wrote with panache. She knew how to set a scene and to tell a story—and she had stories to tell.

In her memoir, Grace tells us about her pioneer forebears, starting with John Kincaid and his wife Eliza McLeese Kincaid, who emigrated from Dublin to Virginia, and whose son David Ingram Kincaid fought in the Civil War on the side of the Confederacy and then married and took home to Columbia, Tennessee, the 13-year-old niece of President Rutherford B. Hayes—the intrepid Rebecca Ann Hayes. As a young widow, Ann heads west across the Plains in a Conestoga wagon with her three children, braving Indians and tornadoes, finally settling in Denver around 1875. There, her daughter Adelaide marries Mills Hamilton Smith and has two daughters: Laura Pearl and our memoirist Grace Ruby[1]—her mother's "jewels." Grace grows up a tomboy in Denver, and then moves to Chicago as a young woman to study voice in hopes of becoming an opera singer. Instead, she marries the delightful Charles Frederic Mather Smith, 20 years her senior, and the newly-weds improbably make their winter home in rural Oakland, Florida, on the southern shore of Lake Apopka, when

---

1. In her memoir, Grace never mentions her second given name, which apparently was never used.

Central Florida was still a primeval jungle teeming with wild animals and exotic flora—a veritable Garden of Eden—just beginning to be tamed by homesteading farmers, ranchers and fishermen. It was a far cry from the genteel life she had led in Chicago. As Grace says, it was the hand of Destiny that led her new husband and her to Oakland, where Grace raises her family, shakes up the community, and lives for more than 50 happy years.

As recounted in her memoir, Grace was a devoted wife and mother, a pioneer, a community organizer, an opera singer, a fashion-setter, an antique collector, a midwife, a businesswoman, a philanthropist—and a great beauty whom men found irresistible. (The long list of her admirers includes a banker, a manufacturer of embalming fluids and disinfecting soaps, an importer of Indian fabrics, an English aristocrat, a world champion trick rider, a doctor and an oilman.) Grace was the first woman in Florida to drive a car; the owner of the first telephone and phonograph in Oakland, and of the first bathtub and flushing toilet in Central Florida; and the first person to drive a car to the top of Pike's Peak without a mechanic. As a child, Grace wanted to be the first lady explorer in history.

Grace's voice comes across loud and clear in her memoir. She was flamboyant, theatrical, uninhibited, adventurous, energetic, glamorous, exuberant, unconventional, willful, irrepressible, big-hearted, and generous to a fault. Her memoir quotes family and friends who describe Grace as being "like a thoroughbred horse . . . always out there in the limelight," "born for the concert stage and the opera," "prone to gallivantin' around." To use Grace's own phrase, she "had personality." It should, therefore, come as no surprise that, in her story-telling, she was also prone to exaggeration (why say she was bitten by a mundane tick when it could have been a scorpion?). She was larger than life—a force of nature—and has been likened to Auntie Mame. As Eve Bacon wrote in her book *Oakland—The Early Years*, Grace "hit staid little Oakland" like "a social bombshell."

OAKLAND BEFORE THE BOMBSHELL HIT

In the mid- to late-19th century, there was the Wild West, and in Florida there was the Wild South. Following each of the three Seminole Wars,[2]

---

2. The First Seminole War was fought between 1817 and 1818; the Second, between 1835 and 1842; and the Third, between 1855 and 1858.

pioneers pushed further and further south, laying claim to homesteads and starting cattle ranches and vegetable and citrus farms. Oakland was settled by such pioneers.[3]

In the 1840s, the first white settlers migrated to the rich muck soil surrounding Lake Apopka ("big potato"), then the second largest lake in Florida. Lake Apopka was located in Mosquito County, which took up much of central Florida. When Florida became a state in 1845, Mosquito County was renamed Orange County after the fruit that was its main product, with Orlando as its seat.

In the years before the Civil War, Col. Issac Hudson from Louisiana and Judge James Gamble Speer from South Carolina founded a settlement on the south shore of Lake Apopka, 20 miles due west of Orlando, which they called Oakland because of the abundance of live oak trees in the area. Judge Speer (1820–93) played a leading role in the development of the community for the rest of his life.

After the Civil War, Florida began to boom as settlers moved in to take advantage of the homestead lands offered by the state. Several families moved to Oakland and homesteaded or purchased for cultivation hundreds of acres of virgin land around the south end of Lake Apopka. Oakland became the principal trading and social center in Central Florida.

James Hardy Sadler (1859–1934), who became a pillar of the Oakland community, came to Oakland from South Carolina as a child in the late 1860s. After his father died, his mother sent him to Oakland to live with his grandfather, Judge Speer. Young Jim Sadler took the train as far south as Gainesville, which was the last stop on the line. His grandfather met him there, and it took them four days to travel 100 miles through the forest back to Oakland.

Luther F. Tilden (1834–1929), who was born in Vermont, grew up on a farm in New York State and then migrated to Illinois, moved to the Oakland area with his family in 1877. He purchased 561 acres of land and founded the area that now bears his name: Tildenville.

At the initiative of Judge Speer, between 1879 and 1887 a canal was dredged from the north side of Lake Apopka to Lake Dora, making it

---

3. The following history is taken from *Oakland—The Early Years (A History of Oakland, Fla.)*, by Eve Bacon, The Mickler House Publishers, Chuluota, Florida, 32766 (1974); and from the page on Oakland's history on the Winter Garden Heritage Foundation's website (www.wghf.org). (Grace's daughter Grace Mary gave a copy of *Oakland—The Early Years* to her daughter Jennifer in 1975, noting that Eve—known as 'Eva' at school—Bacon had been one of her classmates in Oakland.)

possible for produce to be shipped from the dock at Oakland through the canal and a chain of lakes, down the Oklawaha River to Welaka on the St. John's River. Once there, the cargo was loaded on boats for onward shipment to Jacksonville and Savannah.

At first, Oakland's pioneers produced cotton and sugar cane, harvested by slaves they brought with them from South Carolina. When a blight destroyed those plants, tomatoes took their place, but they too proved vulnerable to disease; finally, citrus became the principal crop.

While the canal dramatically improved Oakland's ability to transport its fruits and vegetables to market, it was the coming of the railroad that brought Oakland its boom years, from 1886 to 1895.

Encouraged by generous land grants from the State Internal Improvement Board during the early 1880s, railroad construction took off, opening up inland Florida. Peter Demens (who had immigrated from St. Petersburg, Russia, and whose real name was Piotr Alexewitch Dementief) acquired the Orange Belt Railroad, which had a charter to build a railroad from Lake Monroe, near Sanford, to Lake Apopka, a distance of 35 miles. Judge Speer offered Demens 200 acres on the south shore of the lake if Demens would swing the line into Oakland and move the Orange Belt Investment Company and railroad shops there. Demens agreed, and Oakland began to boom. A hotel was built, as were an opera house (also known as the Union Club), stores, a hospital, substantial homes for the railroad's senior managers, and scores of smaller homes for men brought in to work in the railroad shops. A telegraph office and newspaper were established in the town. The first train rolled into Oakland on November 15, 1886.

Demens then extended the line 100 miles southwest to Pinellas Point on the Gulf, where the town was renamed St. Petersburg after his birthplace. The first train reached St. Petersburg on June 8, 1888, completing the Orange Belt line, which was the longest narrow-gauge railroad in the entire country at that time, but the Orange Belt Investment Company that owned the line was bankrupt. Demens' creditors took over the company and moved the company's headquarters and railroad shops out of Oakland. This marked the beginning of Oakland's economic decline.

The townspeople of Oakland voted to incorporate the town in November 1887, but it was not until 1891 that the Florida legislature officially recognized the incorporation.

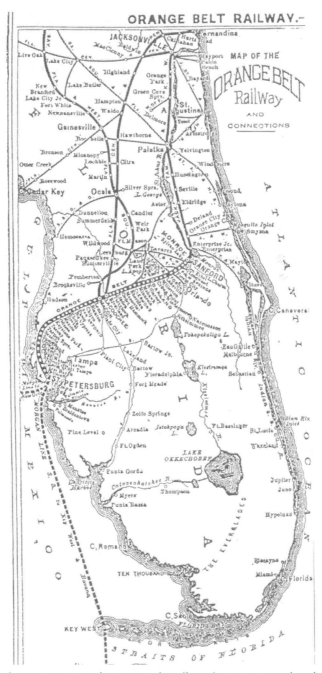

Figure P.1. Map of Orange Belt Railway in 1893. Reproduced courtesy of the Winter Garden Heritage Foundation.

In 1895, the "big freeze" killed most of Florida's citrus groves, so there was almost no freight for the Orange Belt line. Then, in the late 1890s, a disastrous fire completely destroyed Oakland's business district. It was the last straw that broke the economic back of the community. Oakland, led by the Sadlers, the Tildens and other growers, settled back into an agricultural community. From the hustling 1880s and early 1890s, Oakland's population dropped back to around 200 people at the turn of the century.

At the beginning of the twentieth century, Lake Apopka became known as the large-mouth bass fishing capital of the world. At one time, there were around two dozen fish camps on the lake's 40 miles of shoreline, drawing fishermen from around the country. And Fred Mather-Smith liked to fish.

It was at this time that the newly married Grace and Fred Mather-Smith arrived in Oakland.

Acknowledgments

I extend my sincere thanks to Rod Reeves, Kay Cappleman, Jim Crescitelli and the Winter Garden Heritage Foundation for their invaluable assistance in retracing the history of "Miss Grace" in Oakland. The exhibit dedicated to Miss Grace at the Winter Garden Heritage Museum is a fitting tribute to the *grande dame* of Oakland.

Most of all, I wish to thank Grace's daughter Ann, and her granddaughters Jan Ann Turner Detmer, Mary Beth Turner Abel Leeming, Grace Fischbeck Riker, and my mother Jennifer Turner Bailey, for sharing with me their ever vivid memories of her mother and their grandmother. She was one of a kind.

Russell P. Kelley, III

Note from the Editor

I have changed hardly a word of the original manuscript. To make Grace's memoir easier to read, however, I have divided the text into chapters and sub-chapters with titles; added footnotes to supply dates or to identify people and places; changed some punctuation; and sometimes combined two or three short paragraphs into one.

When researching the dates and places of the births and deaths of Grace's forebears, many times I came across slightly different dates or places for the same event. To keep it simple, I picked the most likely dates under the circumstances, without giving the alternatives, and do not guarantee their accuracy.

All photographs are from family collections except those credited to the Winter Garden Heritage Foundation.

The title I have given to Grace's memoir comes from the salutation with which she begins it.

Introduction

My Darlings:

If there must be a reason for that which follows, and it does seem relevant that there should be, then it is because I refuse to go into posterity represented only by a few digits amidst the profusion of statistics that is our genealogy. Even your beloved father will be remembered by the next generation largely by the dates carved on the door of his mausoleum in the garden.

I do not suggest that the small happenings in one's life are individually important, but their total may, to some degree, offer a clue to the blood inheritance from another generation.

After being alone for so long after Father left us, I married Milo McAlpin who is, among other fascinating things, a genealogist of repute.

It distresses me, watching him search through seemingly endless lists of dates in the effort to establish a family's succession, that so seldom is there anything recorded of the lives of the individuals. To be certain, there are brief references to those events of historical importance, but why did not the biographer set down something of the substance of their lives? What of their fortunes and their reverses, their joys, their sorrows and their loves? I prefer not to join this legion.

Should I neglect to record any worthwhile episode within your knowledge, I hasten to say that its absence is not because of a modesty of mine. It is simply that I have forgotten it. Looking back over more than sixty years of my life and far, far more than that of our family's history and legend without some omissions is an improbability.

Chapter One

Arriving in Oakland

At the moment, it seems best to start with the beginning of my life with your father.

We were married in Detroit on May 28th in 1908,[1] by an Episcopalian rector who was a friend of Father's. At eleven o-clock I was Grace Hamilton Smith and at twelve o'clock I was Mrs. Charles Frederic Mather-Smith and we were on the train which was to take us to New York. From there we were to embark at once for a cruise around the world. The honeymoon that I had dreamed of.

Here, with no thought of becoming philosophical, let me say that well-laid plans are wonderful things in an orderly life, but they can be consummated only if they agree with the preordinations of Fate.

Thus we learned, when we reached New York, that the ship which was to take us across the Atlantic was in dry-dock for extensive emergency repairs and that it could not possibly be made ready for the voyage in less than three weeks.

New York in the summer was not to be considered at that time. There was no air-conditioning of course; all the theatres were closed for the summer and even the best restaurants were locked until fall. All who could manage it were away at summer houses.

So Father suggested a coast-wise trip to fill in the time until our sailing. Surely it was the hand of Destiny that ushered us aboard a Clyde Line steamer for Jacksonville that night.[2]

---

1. Actually, Grace was married on June 27, 1908. Throughout her memoir, she is a bit vague on dates, which I try to supply in footnotes.

2. After the Civil War tourism to Florida boomed and Jacksonville became the gateway to the warm winter retreats in Central Florida. Tourists arrived from the north on ocean-going steamers, most of them with a paddle-wheel on each side, called side-wheelers.

Figure 1.1. Map of West Orange County with Oakland on south shore of
Lake Apopka. (Fries, J. O, and E.W. Smith & Co. *Map of Orange County,
Florida*. Philadelphia: E.W. Smith & Co, 1890)

I suspect that Father was secretly glad for this sudden opportunity to
visit Florida once more. He had been there several times before on fishing
expeditions and he loved it. Now we might have time to visit Orlando and
probably acquire a camp near there where we could come later.

The trip down the coast was wonderful. The seas were calm, the
weather perfect and our companions were most delightful. It was not possible, you know, to conceal the fact that we were so newly married—one
never can—so our shipmates devoted themselves to the task of making
us happy and comfortable. They were genuinely regretful that we planned
to disembark at Jacksonville instead of continuing on with them to the
Islands.

I loved Jacksonville,[3] I was enchanted with its quiet southern charm
after the rush and turmoil of Chicago and the hustle-bustle of New York.

3. In 1908, Jacksonville, named after then General Andrew Jackson when Florida became a terri-
tory in 1822, was the largest city in Florida with a population of around 55,000.

From Jacksonville we were to go south by inland steamer,[4] up the St. John's River to Sanford[5] and from there we would proceed by rail to Orlando.

The trip up the river that evening was a journey through fairyland for me. I saw for the first time the huge flights of cormorants hurrying in from the sea to their roosts along the shore for the night, the myriads of ducks in the ponds and eddies, while feeding in the marsh grass were countless great blue and white herons, egrets, cranes, purple grackles and literally clouds of red-wing black birds.

The luxurious side-wheeler which was taking us on our way was so large that now and again the Negro deck hands would go overboard with ropes tied around their middles, swim ashore and snub the boat around the sharper bends. Many times we passed so close to the shore that I could touch the overhanging foliage with my hands.

As we progressed inland away from the sea my fairyland became even more complete. Here, among the palms and the immense pines that had looked upon Ponce de Leon's optimistic explorers, among the tremendous water oaks that had sheltered the pirate crews of long ago and some of which undoubtedly had served as hanging posts for their victims, were the blue-jays, the mockingbirds and the royal red cardinals rejoicing in their evening songs. It was a fairyland indeed.

We had planned that Sanford was merely to be a stopping-off place on our trip south, but again Fate had contrariwise plans. For it was at the hotel in Sanford that we met Mr. Shupneck. We were fascinated by this immensely wealthy, exuberant man who was possessed of an idiosyncrasy for wearing frightfully shiny celluloid collars together with almost equally shiny black ties, both of which you forgot after a minute or two under the spell of his bewitching enthusiasm.

Mr. Shupneck was a self-appointed goodwill emissary for the State of Florida with a boiling passion for interesting others in its future pos-

---

4. At Jacksonville, most passengers transferred to smaller stern-wheelers, which could maneuver in very shallow water. In the late 19th century, there were 150 steamships operating on the St. John's River.

5. According to a 1902 schedule, the Clyde Line side-wheeler *City of Jacksonville* made the 165-mile trip from Jacksonville to Sanford in 17 hours. The St. John's (now Johns) River is 310 miles long and is the longest river in Florida; it is one of the few rivers in the United States flowing north. The St. Johns River has been a vital link between north and central Florida since the 16th century. The river made possible the development of Florida's interior, allowing farmers to transport their crops to Jacksonville, where they would be loaded onto ocean-going ships for sale in the northeast.

sibilities. He wore a cloak like a melodramatic villain and it was rumored that its lining was stitched with packets of paper money so that he might always be prepared to take advantage of an unexpected opportunity.

We were delighted with his habit of pretending to divulge a secret. He would brush his sparse hair across his pate from ear to ear, peer over his glasses in every direction as if to insure privacy, then bellow the secret so that it surely could be heard by the cab drivers in the street below.

Mr. Shupneck did not disparage Orlando. In fact, he was most enthusiastic concerning its probable growth. But such was the wizardry of his words that it was no trick at all for him to convince Father that the country around Oakland, and not Orlando, was the place for us to investigate.

We never had heard of Oakland, nor could we locate anyone around the hotel who had been there. But so effective was Mr. Shupneck that early morning found us on the way to the railroad station and Oakland.

We discovered at once that the daily train inland was most certainly no luxury flier. Besides a couple or three freight cars, it sported a combination passenger, baggage and mail car. The passenger department, we also discovered, was that part of the baggage area supplying enough boxes for seats. The train was powered by a weird-looking, tall-stacked, wood-burning locomotive which must have used prodigious amounts of fuel, for we stopped at frequent intervals to replenish our supply from the stacks in readiness along the track.

We sat in the open doorway on a box of machinery parts for someone's windmill and watched the scenery go by as we ate fresh watermelons—undoubtedly part of a shipment to market.

Again we were passing through a never-never land even more fantastic than the night before. Through a tropical jungle aflame with its mid-summer blooms and virtually alive with story-book creatures. We passed close to marshes where the trees were festooned with huge water snakes intent on the marine life below for their breakfasts. And along lakes where the fish flashed in the morning sun and where alligators sunned themselves on the shores. We saw deer no larger than large dogs and here and there a bear ambled away from the noise of the train. Wild doves shot past us like feathered bullets and turkeys peeped at us from thickets in the distance. Florida primeval, and I loved every foot of it.

After Sanford and Jacksonville had established the pattern in my mind for Florida cities and towns, I was not at all impressed with my first view of Oakland. It was, at first glance, neglected and sprawling, with none of the primness I had expected.

The truth was that the town had passed its hey-day. The railroad shops which had provided a livelihood for a dependent community had been moved to a more fortunate location farther west and a large part of the population had, quite understandably, gone along. The hotel, as a result, was no longer operating, the opera house, where many popular stars had performed, was boarded up, and the church, started long before by the second sons of several English families, had been abandoned. I later acquired its pulpit, rostrum façade and organ for my collection of antiques and relics.

The entire town seemed but a small clearing in the midst of the menacing forest surrounding it. Along the outskirts, where the railroad laborers had lived, the jungle verdure was again encroaching.

The night before we arrived, two marauding panthers had been shot within sight of the post office, and the evening before that alligators had raided the hog pen of a farmer who lived along the lake shore. These events provided news as well as a break in the monotony of the humdrum days for the natives, but I am afraid I had a moment's homesickness for the more familiar furor of Chicago.

My first impression of Oakland was, however, a fleeting one. The town greeted us warmly and at once started to make us comfortable. We found rooms with an English family who were delightful. They took us to their hearts immediately and they were ever so helpful in aiding us to locate a favorable piece of land. There never was a question in their minds but that we were there to stay.

For Father's appetite for fishing, there was Lake Apopka bordering the town on the north. We soon learned from our friends that there was a large tract of land available along its shores.[6] The land had belonged to a family who were unsuccessful with their efforts to raise cotton there. They failed financially and had returned to South Carolina. Father was enthusiastic because the land embraced two flowing wells which, we were assured, had never failed. He bought it without delay.

Time was running dangerously close to the sailing date of our ship for Europe when we both agreed that instead of a camp, we should build a home, and that instead of traveling the world just then, put our roots down

---

6. Forty acres, which Grace and Fred named Edgegrove Farms.

in Florida. So happy were we that each had discovered that the other was contented here that we staged a big party of celebration at our boarding house. We sang and danced all night long.

Now we had the land but no house. With almost no delay we found that the problem of building a home was to be a huge one. Father and I went to Orlando in high spirits to order the materials and arrange for the builders. But there we discovered that not only were adequate materials scarce, but competent workmen were practically non-existent as far as we were concerned. There were few carpenters in town and those few were in such demand that they could neither be coaxed nor bribed into coming way out to Oakland.[7]

From Orlando we hurried to Jacksonville where we found the situation even worse. All available workmen were engaged months in advance. On the return trip to Oakland, Father cheerfully informed me that he did not intend that a handful of autocratic carpenters should alter our decision to remain in Florida—and in our own home.

Again with the help of our kind neighbors, we located a well-built house some distance from town. It was vacant and for sale. Five rooms and solidly built from seasoned cypress, it came close to meeting the specifications we had in mind when we planned to build. The fact that a road must be carved out of the woods to deliver it to our location was an insignificant obstacle compared to the delays of building.

Within a month our new home was set on its new foundation facing the lake. The poor, straining mules that had coaxed and yanked and worried it through the woods were not half as glad as we were when, at last, it was settled in place. We immediately celebrated this event with a house-warming, at which the entire town was present at some time, throughout the night.

So we started our first year together—not with the planned trip around the world in luxury—but under conditions so primitive that they included oil lamps, a cantankerous wood-burning stove and a three-mile daily hike over the sand roads for fresh milk.

By training and experience, it is doubtful if any bride was more poorly equipped for the immediate life ahead than I. But as my mother was later fond of reminding me, "whatever you lacked in the way of personal experience, was more than compensated for by your inheritance of the pioneering spirit of your ancestors."

---

7. Oakland was due west of Orlando, at first accessible by around 25 miles of meandering rough sand roads, and later by a one-lane brick road. On today's roads, Oakland is 20 miles west of Orlando.

Chapter Two

Pioneer Ancestors

JOSEPH AND ELIZA KINCAID

Great-grandfather Joseph Kincaid, born in Dublin, Ireland, was a King's soldier in his youth. It is the prerogative of young men to enjoy soldiering and fighting, and so did Joseph—but he had small liking for the restraints imposed by the Crown. He longed for the life of a free man. As soon as he could obtain his release from the Guard, he married and with his bride, Eliza McLeese, sailed by the earliest possible ship for the free land of America.

Joseph was undoubtedly a happy man now. His wife was acknowledged to be one of the most beautiful women in all Ireland; they were deeply in love and now they were off for the land where no man owed allegiance to another.

Joseph and Eliza settled in Virginia where Joseph again resumed the trade he knew best—that of soldiering. The King had trained his warriors well, for it was not long before he was honored with a commission in the Virginia Militia. He proved to be an exceptional soldier, so he was again promoted—this time to the rank of captain. The records of the State of Virginia disclose that he fought with great distinction throughout the Revolutionary War.

Eliza and Joseph had two sons born to them in Virginia. David Ingram was the older, then Joseph.

DAVID INGRAM KINCAID

Eliza's kin also migrated to this country and they settled in Pennsylvania, so the boys grew up to have many friends in the north as well as the south. David, with his yearning to explore as much of the country as possible, travelled on horseback from Virginia to New York and then as far west as the Ohio River, making friends wherever he stopped. One of his closest ones was Rutherford Birchard Hayes, who was destined to become a President of the United States.

The continued travels of the two boys explains why, at the start of the War between the States, Joseph found himself on the side of the Union while David, then in Virginia, joined the forces of the South.

Family legend is somewhat obscure as to the details, but somehow the two brothers met on the field of battle.

David had little difficulty convincing Joseph that not only was he likely to see more action than him, but also that Joseph rightfully belonged with the Army of the South. Without further ceremony, the brothers stripped the grey uniform from a fallen soldier and Joseph became a member of the Confederacy. Together they fought long and well until Joseph was killed in an heroic battle near Columbia.[1] There is a monument in Kentucky honoring the Kincaid brothers.

At the conclusion of the war, David, with a group of forty-nine of his men, wandered about seeking a suitable place to start life anew. Finally, they crossed the Duck River into Tennessee and settled the village that is now Columbia.

Mature and enlightened now, David longed, not for more travel or fighting, but for a more constructive life than he had had as a soldier. After much hesitation he decided to become a preacher.

He had not reckoned with the reactions of his men, however. They had known him only as a hard-fighting soldier, with all of the talents that made him a leader under fire. They remembered his great facility with the wounded and ill on the battlefield and it seemed logical that he develop his talents along that line. They urged him to reconsider and become their doctor. David was adamant—he would not change his decision. But as

---

1. The Battle of Columbia (Tennessee) was fought between November 24 and 29, 1863.

a preacher, the men would have none of him. They ridiculed him to the point where he found it wise to leave the community for a time.

He saddled his horse and started for a visit to some of his friends in the north. Finally, he rode to Chillicothe, Ohio, for the counsel of President Hayes.[2]

REBECCA ANN HAYES

Now again Destiny manifests itself. For Rebecca Ann, a niece of the President's, was staying at the Hayes home. David, although a handsome man, had not been impressed with any girl until now. But he lost his heart to Rebecca Ann at first sight and he refused to leave for the South without her.

In the present age of genuflection to the conventions, it is startling to remember that the girl was but thirteen years old at the time. However, they were married with the unstinted blessing of the Hayes family. They left immediately after the wedding for Columbia, carrying with them only what they could manage on horseback.

That trip must have been a hard one for a bride and groom. The roads toward the South were badly neglected because of the war and the impoverished condition of the states afterward. Safe and adequate accommodations were so scarce that at times they were forced to sleep in the fields or in barns along the way. For food, they depended upon David's gun and his knowledge of roots and berries. An additional hazard was presented by the marauding bandit bands infesting the districts around the highways. But David was a resourceful man as well as a fine one in a fight, so in the end he brought his bride safely to Columbia.

Now David heeded the earlier advice of his companions—that he become a doctor. He added to his war experiences with the wounded by study and reading. He learned the mysteries of birth from long observation of the animals in the fields; he travelled to the Indians to augment his already considerable knowledge of herbs and purges; and he became proficient in blood-letting, an art which had long been practiced by the

---

2. Rutherford B. Hayes was Governor of Ohio from 1868 to 1872, and again from 1876 to 1877; he was President of the United States from 1877 to 1881.

barbers of that and earlier days. At length he became a reputable doctor with a practice that continued to grow until his death.

David built the ancestral home in Columbia, and it would be most gratifying now to say that David and Rebecca Ann, with their growing family of four children, led completely happy lives there ever after.

But as a matter of truth, Ann could not have been serenely happy in Columbia. She was, after all, a Yankee coming into the South at a time when feelings were highly opinionated. And she came as the wife of a highly desirable man for whom many of the girls of the town had set their caps.

Ann adored David and she was happily content with him, but the community did not accept her. For years she was ostracized with no friends among her neighbors. David begged her to consent to leave the place forever in favor of some place in the North, but she would not agree. "Moving away will not change their feelings a bit," she would say. "They really hurt themselves more than they injure me. No, David, the children are happy here, so here we stay."

Years later, when feelings softened and society tried to make amends, she no longer cared.

ADELAIDE ELIZA KINCAID

The children were indeed happy in Columbia. The cause of the parental feud was too intangible for the next generation to understand, so the Kincaid children were popular with their schoolmates. The two brothers, Sam and James, had many friends, while their sisters, Laura Pearl and Adelaide Eliza, were practically besieged by the young men of the neighborhood, as well as by some who were not so young.

At sixteen, Adelaide was easily the most popular young lady in town. She had many suitors, among them a widower named William Howard. Mr. Howard owned large tracts of land in and around Columbia as well as a diversity of interests in local industries. He was considered to be a wealthy man and, as such, he was looked upon with favor by Adelaide's parents. She, however, found it difficult to take him seriously because he had daughters who not only were her friends, but who were older than she. David and Ann were insistent and finally she became engaged to him for an early marriage although she was frank in declaring that she did not love him.

Adelaide seldom spoke of that wedding day. When she did, it was to recall her terror as she arranged her wedding gown. At the last minute, her courage failed her and she dashed from the house and the assembled guests, mounted the nearest horse at the hitching rack outside the door and galloped madly across the fields, her gown snagging on the tumbleweed in her path.

Her mount was poorly chosen in her haste, so the groom and the pursuing guests soon outrode her. She was brought back like a truant child and the ceremony was performed. She never was happy as Mrs. Howard.

Adelaide's husband was not a temperate man, and this, together with his unhappy marriage and a series of unwise manipulations concerning his business interests, caused his health to fail rapidly. Soon he died, his fortune dissipated with the exception of his debt-burdened lands. The girl who had not wanted to leave home in the first place now returned to it a widow. Instead of the riches she might have enjoyed, she became a school teacher, and a teacher she remained until her father died.

When Mr. Howard's lands increased in value and were sold for the phosphate deposits discovered there, his children offered Adelaide a share in the profits from their sale, but she refused.

It was an axiom in those days that ill-luck in a family—but never good fortune—always occurred in threes. And so it did with the Kincaid family. First Adelaide became a widow, then Laura died—then David.

WESTWARD HO!

With David gone and her family no longer youngsters, Ann found Columbia less attractive than ever. I am sure it was with mingled feelings that she now decided to leave it forever. Certainly she was glad to leave, at long last, the community that had ignored her when she needed their friendship so urgently. On the other hand, she was departing from the scenes of her many happy years with David.

Figure 2.1. Rebecca Ann Hayes Kincaid

But Ann, although deeply religious, was never a sentimentalist. She gave the house and land to Adelaide, then locked it up, bought a broad-wheeled, covered Conestoga wagon and the mules to draw it, and with her family of three she headed west with no particular destination in mind. Mother often told me that Ann never looked behind her that whole first day. Her life lay ahead.

That was another trip of Destiny. Ann had not intended to travel to Denver. She vaguely planned to settle in one of the Plains states. But she did migrate to Colorado, the size of her family again diminished by one, and at her journey's end, Adelaide was to meet her future husband.

What a trip that must have been for the Kincaids. Again let me lament the fact that there are no detailed records of their trials among the family papers. Merely the memories recounted for me by Ann many years later, for Ann became my grandmother.

The family progressed with painful slowness across two-thirds of the State of Tennessee—ferried across the Mississippi River where they almost lost two of their mules overboard when they were struck by another barge, and then across the almost unpopulated breadth of lower Missouri and into Kansas.

They replenished their water barrels and watered the animals at creeks and rivers whenever they could, but all through the Plains they had to depend on the wells of the widely scattered homesteaders. Ann developed a goiter from the strain of continued pumping that tormented her for the rest of her life.

Ann was a pioneer and she knew all the laws of self-preservation. Every few hours she would climb onto the top of the covered wagon and scan the country in every direction for a warning of possible trouble. And she found it, too.

Dust on the horizon might herald the welcome meeting with another traveller or caravan; it might foretell a coming storm; or what was more likely and least welcome, warn them of the near presence of a raiding Indian band. The Blackfeet often crossed the Missouri River to the north of their route. They foraged as far south as the Arkansas [River]. Wagon trains always assumed in advance that there were no peaceful Indians. At the first sign of a roving band, the trains prepared at once to fight or flee. A single wagon must always evade them, if possible.

So when Ann discovered smoke against the sky-line one morning, she halted and sent Sam ahead with David's old spy-glass to determine its cause while she hid the rest of the family in a thicket. Sam reported that a large band of Indians had killed a buffalo for breakfast and were feasting; the smoke was from their cook-fire.

Feverishly they unloaded the wagon with the exception of a few pieces not likely to interest the Indians, then drove it about a mile from the thicket. It required the efforts of the entire family to overturn the wagon in an exposed spot. Then Ann hid the family and the mules among the bushes, with David's mules loaded and ready.

The ruse worked. The Blackfeet sent a party ahead to investigate and, evidently assuming that another band had looted the wagon and carried its occupants off with them, continued on toward Missouri. They did not bother to burn the wagon. The family remained hidden for most of that day before they dared to approach the wagon.

The following morning they awakened to find several Indians standing silently only a short distance away. Ann jumped for the muzzle loader just as the leader called to her. They were friendly and they needed salt. Ann also doctored one of them who had been shot through the leg. Whenever she told me of this episode, she would brush her hands together with distaste and declare that she could smell him for a month afterwards.

When their water barrel sprung a leak, the little remaining liquid was saved for the mules while the family did without for three days except for what little they could collect on their tarpaulins spread carefully to collect the night's dew.

They ate cold food or none at all whenever they feared that a fire might divulge their location to the Indians. They wallowed through ankle-deep mud after a torrential rain, and they sat huddled against the wagon with their tarpaulins covering them for an entire day while the sky turned black and a dust storm tried its best to either bury them alive or suffocate them.

Another day, glimpsing the black clouds racing up behind them, Ann tried to reach the comparative shelter of a homesteader's home just visible in the distance ahead. But they could not reach it before the storm was upon them. They tied the mules to a tree and tied the wagon to another, then lashed themselves to still another. They lay face down and prayed to God while a tornado swept everything before it to destruction only a few feet away. Its force drove tiny twigs into the trunks of the trees about them like nails and deposited a wagon box and a man's hat from goodness knows where on the trail just ahead.

When the storm passed, the settler's house was gone and they found its occupants dead—still lashed to their bedstead—a half mile beyond. Ann, with her family as mourners, said a prayer over them and then buried them where their doorstep had been. They left a note of explanation for their neighbors and went on.

The two women remained at the shack of a homesteader while the two boys backtracked fifty miles to replace one of their mules that had stepped into a hole and broken his leg. After the boys left, Ann discovered that the homesteader was demented because of the recent death of his wife. She insisted that she never closed an eye until Sam and James returned although the man did not try to harm them.

They camped under the blazing sun for a week while a friendly traveller brought them a replacement for a broken wheel; and they went forward under starvation rations after an unfriendly one stole most of their food at a portage.

Surely a less determined woman than Ann would have turned back in the face of these adversities. And a less adventurous trio than Adelaide, James and Sam would have insisted on it. But in spite of everything, they liked both Missouri and Kansas.

Ann bought vast tracts of land as they went along. Land, soon to command fabulous prices because of the discovery of oil beneath it, could be had for a dollar an acre. And land that was to produce the world's finest corn sold for even less than that.

Ann declared that Kansas was the end of the long trail. Certainly the fantastically rich soil could not be equaled anywhere on this continent. Further, the steadily increasing number of migrants exploring the possibilities in Kansas would increase land values tremendously. Ann prayed to her God for guidance and bought more land.

She wanted to give each of the boys a tract to develop for his own but Sam would not accept his. He had no desire to become a farmer. He was content to stay and help the others get started but he wanted to move on eventually. He talked of hitching a ride back to Columbia with a passing wagon train or of buying a horse and a saddle to take him to St. Louis or Chicago—anywhere where there were plenty of lights and people.

James was happy with his land and started to clear and break it for plowing at once. He drove for miles to visit his neighbors and to learn from them the likely crops and the possible markets.

Soon he was courting the daughter of a farmer from the Smoky Hill River region to the north. This was an eventuality that was not a part of Ann's plans. To make matters worse, she did not like the girl. But she could not influence James' heart, although she tried. When they were married, she was, in her own words, "plain disgusted with it all."

So much so, in fact, that again she loaded the wagon and, with Adelaide and happy Sam, started westward once more, buying more land wherever it seemed wise as they went along.

Eventually, when oil was discovered on James' land and he became wealthy, she was pleased over his good fortune but she never changed her opinion of his wife, and so far as I know she never saw her again.

As the Kincaids travelled west along the Arkansas River, Ann began to hear tales of the riches of Colorado. Gold has been discovered there and copper, lead and mica were being mined in quantity. Discounting for the enthusiasm of the hopefuls who told the stories, Ann recognized the opportunities for the early birds.

Now, for the first time since leaving Columbia, they had a definite destination.

They left the river valley to head north and west over a vaguely defined route, and soon there were new hardships to be encountered and overcome. First there were hills which tired the mules; then came the mountains that almost killed them with exhaustion. Poor trails and, in places, no trails at all.

Where the way was too steep, they unloaded the wagon—sometimes five or six times in one day—and hauled their supplies up, a few pieces at a time. There were days when they could still see their starting point at sundown.

There were nights when they took turns staying awake to keep fires blazing on either side of them to keep from freezing. Boulders stalled the wagon and they felled saplings to prize it over them. Rattlesnakes bothered them in their camps, and they had to learn to sleep with packs of howling coyotes trying their best to keep them awake.

But they reached Denver just before winter set in. The stories they had heard were not just embellished tales. They were true to the last word. Here was an unbelievable country. Wealth lay everywhere, it seemed. But there was a panic in the East. Money was tight and work was scarce as a result. Mines were idle for the want of operating capital; the refineries were silent. It was a situation made to order for Ann. Mines as well as mining sites were available for cash. So again they bought.

Ann decided that here, in truth, was the end of the long trail for the Kincaids. Denver would be their home.

She sold the mules and the faithful wagon to a family of die-hards who were heading for California, unloaded David's musket and moved her family to an hotel.

MILLS HAMILTON SMITH

Now my story must go back for a bit to tell you about Mills Hamilton Smith, the man who was to be my father.

How did Destiny go about the business of bringing together a young man from along the Mississippi River in Kentucky and a young widow from Columbia, Tennessee? By the simple expedient of directing each of them to Denver, Colorado.

Mills' father, James Augustus Smith, was the grandson of Randolf Smith, an English barrister who migrated from his homeland to settle in Lexington, Kentucky.

After James' marriage, he lived for some time in the town of Cleves, in Hamilton County, Ohio. Here Mills and his brother [William] Cleves[3] were born. When the boys were very small, James moved back to Kentucky. There James owned and operated a freight landing as well as a number of river boats which delivered freight up and down the Mississippi.

Mills' father did not believe in the practice—which was quite in vogue at that time—that a son with expectations might manage with a minimum of work until he inherited a business from his father. Contrariwise, it was his conviction that opportunities in this country were so numerous and varied that a young man should be exposed to them with parental help.

---

3. Born on January 6, 1858.

Accordingly, when Mills and Cleves were old enough, he supplied each with a sum of money and left them free to decide where each would choose to try for his fortune.

It is odd that each one should elect to engage in the business of buying and selling real estate, although not together. Cleves settled in St. Louis while Mills Hamilton went on to Denver, envisioning the possibilities there.

Aside from its business advantages, Denver was a wise choice for Mills. He never was a robust man and the high altitude was a tonic for him. Before long he had his own office and gradually he came to handle mining properties only. It was because of a transaction concerning a mica-bearing property that he met my mother.

Ann had shrewdly completed a deal for the property which a group of eastern investors, represented by Mills, were most anxious to acquire. Her advantage of an immediate cash payment, while Mills had to wait for instructions from his principals, got her the land for an amount below the original asking price. Mills called at the hotel to meet the astute business woman who has bested him, and there he met Adelaide.

Mother never said very much about her engagement to Mills. She believed that romance was a personal affair. They must have been attracted to each other at once however, for they were married within a few months.[4]

---

4. They probably married in 1877 since their first child was born in their first year of marriage and their second child Laura was born in 1879.

Chapter Three

Denver

Their first child, a boy, was born within the first year of their marriage, but he did not live. Then my sister Laura Pearl came to them. Before I was born, five years after Laura Pearl, another son was born and died at birth.

Adelaide still owned the home in Columbia, of course, and she and Ann made infrequent trips there. I do not believe that Mills ever accompanied them. He loved Denver and there is no question but what the climate there was beneficial to his sometimes precarious health. However, when I was on the way to coming into this world, Mother was insistent that I be born, as was she, in Columbia. She and Father planned to go home together for the event.

Figure 3.1.   Grace at age 3

Maybe it was not Fate this time—it may have been only my personal willfulness—but Mother's bags were all packed and Father was at the office making last minute business arrangements when I upset all of the careful plans by arriving far ahead of the calculated schedule. So instead of becoming Mother's first Columbia baby, I was born as 3203 Arapahoe Street in Denver, Colorado.[1]

I do not think that Mother ever fully forgave me, for she often told me that there definitely was something wrong with a girl who, with a choice in the matter, would deliberately prefer not to be born in Tennessee.

I wish so much that I might record here a great deal more about my father for he must have been an interesting man, with an energy difficult to understand in one so unwell.

His photographs disclose that he was slight, very erect and with dark hair and brown eyes. He wore the full spike moustache so popular at that time. His own business profitable, he was equally successful managing properties for others. He was a firm believer in the advantages of a business education for young people, so he started a business school as a side occupation. The first in the United States. He was an expert penman. I have in my bedroom a scroll executed by him that rivals a steel engraving.

He was extremely devoted to my mother and she found in him all of the love, comfort and companionship so sadly lacking in her earlier marriage.

Father died of pneumonia when he was but thirty-six years old. I was but twenty-one months old at the time[2] so I have no personal memory of him whatsoever.

After Father's death, Mother was disconsolate. She affected mourning in his memory as was proper at that time, but she wore it far, far longer than custom dictated. She also decreed it for Laura and me. I know that I wore mourning for a father that I did not remember until I started to school. Mother, however, still wore black after I had grown up and married. I distinctly remember buying her a respectably dark green dress when we were in Chicago. Her first bit of color since Father's death. She was extremely timid about wearing it outside the house. She said it made her feel like a brazen hussy. Mother also kept Father's slippers, his pipe and his smoking jacket in their accustomed place for years.

During the next few years, we spent more time at our house in Columbia. Mother seemed to want to get away from the more intimate memories.

I loved the old home, with its huge, rambling rooms and hallways; the yard, shaded by the old oaks and chinaberry trees and the tremendous

---

1. According to her tombstone, Grace was born on May 4, 1884.
2. So Mills would have died around January 1886.

magnolia that Ann had planted as a bride. The old hitching rack from which Adelaide had snatched a horse for that desperate flight was also there, but I did not know its story then.

And I had many friends in Columbia; girls whose friendship I still cherish and, as I grew older, boys. Mother insisted that I was even more popular that she had been. But she had learned a terrible lesson in Columbia so her supervision was most exact.

Each time we visited Columbia, Mother bemoaned the changing landscape. The lazy roadway that had wandered conveniently close to the doorsteps of the various plantations to the south, wherever they might be located, was being relocated to provide a shorter route into town. The plantations themselves were disappearing one by one. Phosphate deposits had been discovered underlying the entire section and the land was being purchased for that mineral.

At last, Mother could no longer hold out against the offers of the chemical companies and she sold. Denver became our only home.

My recollection of the first few years of my life is a rather dim one as far as actual occurrences are concerned; no doubt because nothing of much importance happened to me. It is reasonable to assume, however, that I did not run too wild and free.

Both Mother and Grandma were deeply religious. In addition, they had been born to a rapidly outdating moral code which not only guided all of their actions, but somehow reached out to include me as well. Fundamentally, its theory was that if a child's playtime was quite freely sprinkled with household duties, then dusting, dishwashing, darning and mending—even knitting and fancy work—automatically became a sort of game and the child grew up to appreciate the seriousness of life and to classify the shallowness of its pitfalls. A beautiful and Elysian theory that allowed for no measure of human frailty.

Certainly Mother could not be blamed too much. She had had Laura five years before me and Laura's temperament was such that she actually enjoyed doing all these things. My blood mixture was slightly different though—perhaps a little more of grandpa David. I was an experimenter.

Because of the penalties involved—and Grandma particularly was never to be under-rated—I dutifully performed my tasks, but no one ever could make me like them. Nor, whenever there seemed to be an even chance of not getting caught, was I above sneaking out of them.

Once when I was supposed to be on the front porch darning some of my stockings, I could not resist the lure of a ride on a passing ice wagon with its tempting step, dripping with ice water, on the rear. When I returned, there was Grandma on the porch, mending my stockings. I have long since forgotten what wild tale I told her. She abhorred a lie so she took me into the kitchen and washed my mouth out with soft soap. Our laundry soap was homemade from waste fats and home-produced lye. The lye was formed by leaching out wood ashes with rainwater and soft soap was developed by using an extra amount of lye to prevent the soap from hardening. You can imagine the condition of my mouth for several days after that treatment.

Another time, instead of dusting a dark and dreary parlor, I chose to interview the men who were painting the house instead. I climbed the ladder and was having a grand time on the swinging plank when Grandma (who was supposed to be napping, but wasn't) caught me red-handed. That time, she took down my pants right in front of the painters and took their paddle to me—paint and all.

On still another occasion, no doubt around the Fourth of July, I exploded a cannon cracker under a passing horse and buggy. After he got his horse under control, the man grabbed me, placed me on the seat alongside him and drove me about three miles into the country. "Now walk home," he said, "and all the way home reflect on what a bad girl you have been."

SCHOOL DAYS

One might suppose that I would look forward to my first school year but I did not. It may have been my sub-conscious, resenting in advance the new restrictions about to be imposed on my free time. I am sure that many have gone into prison for the rest of their lives with less fuss that I made the morning that Mother took me by the hand to enroll me. I recall that I was close to hysterics because I could not take "Sant," my Saint Bernard companion since babyhood, to class with me.

But I was wrong about school, as always I have been wrong in forming an opinion without first knowing all the facts. I liked my companions at once and, strangely, I was fond of my classroom studies. The first two or three years were a complete success. Then came the beginning of the homework and this I resented mightily. It was assigned by the ream each day and I looked upon it as an unjustified punishment.

Laura, who was my idol, tried her best to make me understand its importance. Under her watchful eye I often prepared it with care and precision. Not so much to increase my knowledge but rather to please my sister. Because I was not prepared each day, it seemed to me that the only times I was ever called upon to recite were those times when I was not ready. It is easy to understand that I came to suspect a conspiracy against me, and it is equally easy to see why my teachers began to form some rather definite conclusions concerning me.

"Superficial studying"—"no real interest." "She learns easily and quickly in class but she will not apply herself—she skips the important things" was the gist of their complaints to Mother. And to a remarkable degree, they were right, although I never could admit that at home.

It is more than possible that poor Miss Mallory wished fervently that I was in darkest Africa instead of Denver, while I, in turn, wished her to a far less fascinating place. Africa was one of my favorite places; perhaps I should head an expedition there someday. The first lady explorer in history.

I am sure that the dear lady was hastened toward her grave by my continued indifference as to whether Cuba was located at eight-two degrees west longitude or twenty-eight degrees east. Whether James Monroe was the fifth President of the United States or the sixth did not seem to me to be of earth-shaking importance either.

Even my answers concerning Abraham Lincoln were never correct because they were not the ones in the history book. My knowledge of Lincoln was largely first hand and much more colorful than the written record. I had got it from Grandma.

I presume that it was in desperation and with relief that I was passed from grade to grade with such prompt regularity, although the heritage that I carried with me each time never served to endear me to the new teacher. Usually they were prepared to dislike me in advance and I detested most of them.

With the exception, of course, of Miss Rand. Miss Rand—I can't remember that anyone ever knew her first name—tried so hard to instruct us in singing.

She was a huge, middle-aged woman with perpetually sore feet and a fuzzy mole on her chin. And she had the voice of an angel. But a tiny angel. It is difficult to describe her singing voice. It was bird-like and sweet—with but a fraction of the volume one would expect from one of such gargantuan proportions.

Miss Rand was my first ideal aside from my sister. I loved to sing and she recognized that fact. And because of it, she had a special liking for me. Quite early she was sure of the possibilities in my voice. Finally she called on Mother to impress upon her the importance of voice education for me. "She will truly go far. She is a lovely child and will grow into a beautiful woman," said Miss Rand to Mother. "She can be a great opera star while she is still very young if you start now."

Mother was impressed with all of it except the "opera star" part. The theatre was a fleshpot of the devil, according to her religious beliefs. In addition, it reminded her of a family skeleton which she did not want to remember. I shall tell you about that presently.

Grandma was no less devout than Mother, but she could find a tiny loophole in her convictions that separated the opera from other theatre activities. She was delighted and, with her usual proclivity for getting things done in a hurry (a trait I think some of you have accused me of inheriting from her), wanted to get out and find me a teacher.

Mother was more basic. She realized that my formal education—dismal as the prospect might be—could not be put aside for a musical one, especially when the obvious goal was the theatre. The net result was that Grandma was voted down and I did not get my singing lessons just then.

The lessons did start sooner than I had expected, however, and most likely my being taken out of public school permanently by Mother was the indirect cause of my getting them.

That year I, along with the rest of the class, was exposed to the mechanical precision of Miss Miller. She was a worshiper of dogma. No deviation from the printed word was permitted under any circumstances. Recitations to her became feats of memory; free interpretation was a heinous offense. "The authority had a specific reason for stating it precisely that way. Do you presume to know better than he?" That and similar admonitions did not impress me to the same degree as they did the others. The result was that I spent more than a little time in the office of the principal.

Our principal was, as I suppose many of the poor souls are, an eternally tormented diplomat. She vacillated between sympathy for me when we were alone, and bruskness toward me whenever a teacher or parent was present. I know I should have been bewildered by such treatment; instead, I merely accepted it.

In these enlightened days, school systems have more scientific means for determining the worth of a teacher, but then it was the custom for the school director to visit each classroom near the end of the term and, by listening to the class perform, presumably judge that teacher's effectiveness.

Miss Miller, with her reputation thus at stake, certainly should have known better than to call upon me with all of those dignitaries present, but call on me she did. I know now that I invited quick strangulation when I told the assembly that I neither knew nor cared whether Charlemagne was the father or the son of Pepin the Short. I can still hear the thunder of the silence that followed.

My days at school became more and more difficult after that and shortly before the end of that term Mother removed me from public school permanently after a memorably strenuous session with most of the faculty.

I was then enrolled in a convent in Denver. Or rather, in the parochial school presided over and taught by the nuns from the adjoining convent. And there, I was completely happy.

We obeyed the rigid rules—far more strict than those at public schools, without question—in return for the friendly understanding of our teachers. We were encouraged in self-interpretation and guided gently back toward the truth when we started astray.

Mother Borgia was a wonderful person, but to me, a Protestant, just a little awesome. I attended prayers with the rest of the girls each day, a period which caused me some anxiety at first. I did so want everything to remain so beautifully perfect that I was trembling with apprehension when I approached Mother Borgia with the problem the prayers presented. I told her that I was not a Catholic and that we had not prayed at the other school although the teacher read a short prayer each morning. Therefore might I be excused from prayers here.

"You may do just as you wish, my dear," she told me. "Certainly you need not go to prayers if you would rather not. But you do learn prayers in your church, do you not?" I told her that I had learned several prayers.

"Then why not go to the chapel with the other girls and repeat your own prayers to yourself. After all, that is what your classmates are doing. Just saying their own prayers." The solution was so simple that I could hardly believe it. After that, I went to chapel with the others, and from the repetition of my prayers I got to know their true meaning. As long as I attended classes at the convent no one ever tried, by word or action, to alter my religious beliefs in any way.

If there was a favorite among my teachers, it was Sister Cecelia, our instructress in music. She was most pleased with my voice and as soon as she recognized the possibilities she too called on Mother to advise her that I should be trained outside the school.

I suppose this advice, coming from the good sister, gave Mother a picture of me singing in some great church, for now she agreed to find me a competent teacher. Now my happiness was complete. Then Uncle Jim visited us and upset my life again.

Grandma consulted Uncle Jim on business matters from time to time and, at long intervals, he came to see us in Denver. This time he was aghast at the news of my attending the convent. He was a most strongly opinionated non-Catholic, so he was positive that the motive behind my teacher's kindnesses to me was to painlessly swerve me toward the Catholic faith. Ridiculous, of course, and cruel, but he was so emphatic that Mother finally agreed to take me out of the convent and to depend on private tutors after that.

She advertised for a tutor only to learn that the only instructors available in the city were public school teachers who gave private instructions afternoons and on Saturdays. Mother enrolled me with Mrs. Anderson's Latin School.

Actually, while Latin was the main course, the school was a sort of finishing school for adolescents and youngsters. We were instructed in the social graces with special emphasis on lady-like deportment. This last course was something less than a success, however, for many reasons. The darling Mrs. Anderson should have realized that it takes longer than a school term to make a lady.

Although a friend and I were very popular throughout the term, the class, including my friend, certainly tried to make my graduation a memorable one. The girls circulated the edict that there were to be no flowers for the students at graduation. Then, on the big afternoon, as we marched through the auditorium to the platform, each girl's parents presented her with a bouquet—except mine, of course.

The trick was intended to embarrass me out of countenance. But I had long since learned to expect the unexpected at unexpected times, so I smiled convincingly and spoke my piece and sang my Latin solo as if nothing unusual had occurred.

Mrs. Anderson told Mother after the ceremonies that she had never been so proud of anyone and that her judgement was that I was the only one in the entire class who had not flunked the course in proper deportment.

SINGING LESSONS

In the meantime, Mother had not gone back on her word to provide singing lessons. She enrolled me with Professor Armando Ciaffano, obviously an Italian, who was the foremost singing teacher in the city at the time.

I am sure that the professor was an influence in my life if he did no more than to strengthen my determination, although he did much more for me than that.

He was possessed of all of the charm of his race and he seemed to live only for his music. He was so gracious when he told me, after a few lessons, that I would not make a great singer, that I could not be angry.

Professor Ciaffano belonged to the era when opera singers, more often than not, resembled pachyderms and had lungs of leather. My slight figure and my timidity in the presence of this great man did not add up to the necessary qualities for greatness for him, I thought.

"You do not eat right, no?" he thundered at me. "You do not eat right, you cannot sing right. The face, she is beautiful—too beautiful; but the body—Pah. Puny! No wonder you tire so quick," and he would shake his fierce black hair and look so distressed that I wanted to agree with him.

But in spite of his obvious convictions, he was a thorough workman. I insisted on staying on with him and he, in turn, gave full value for every dollar we paid him. Gradually he strengthened my lung power, he kept me from straining my voice trying to emulate his immense power, and he taught me to breathe correctly.

"Especially not too soft, you should not sing," he would instruct. Then with a shrug, "Of course, not too loud either—but never too soft. Soft singing tells you are afraid is not perfect."

A word of praise from him and I would practice far into the night.

GROWING UP

At the same time, I was growing up. I had long since outgrown the period of the famous red dress that Grandma insisted that I wear around the house. That dress was a hideous thing as I remember it now. Then, it was merely a nuisance. It was a long, almost shapeless tube reaching almost to my shoetops, with wrist length sleeves, a ruffle around the neck and a deeper one at the hem. And it was red wool—an uninteresting dull brick red.

Grandma, I believe, had some idea that such a dress would instill modesty and otherwise keep me on a straight and narrow path. She never did know how easily—and incidentally, how immodestly—the ruffle at the bottom could be hoisted waist high when we climbed fences or shinnied up trees for a neighbor's apples.

Nor did the dress interfere unduly the day I had the fight with Roscoe Livermore. To this day I cannot recall the circumstances leading up to the fight, but I do remember the battle. Roscoe was a nice boy and one of my puppy admirers, but I never could abide his name. At play I could call him Monk, and that was all right, but at parties or at school where I had to address him as Roscoe, I rebelled. Perhaps that is why we fought. I recall that I won, but I always have suspected that it was his chivalry rather than my prowess that decided the outcome. Later, he became a professional prize fighter and a rather good one.

Let me say here that Roscoe was not my only admirer nor was that chastity dress my only garment. The admirers, as individuals, I have forgotten, just as they have undoubtedly forgotten me. But I do remember some of the dresses. I had one dimity print dress with tiny baskets of flowers sprinkled all over it in a pattern. For parties and for calling with Mother, that was a favorite. Until one evening at an ice cream social held on Beatty's side lawn. Lawn socials like that one, are a never-to-be-experienced thrill in this age. Held in the cool of the evening on a spacious lawn, with paper

Japanese lanterns candle-lighted and hung in strings from tree to tree with long festoons of crepe paper streamers hung in between, and benches and chairs all over the place. And always with a bench or two placed discreetly behind some of the shrubbery.

This particular social was a gala affair. We even had a mandolin and zither trio for the music. Mother, Sister, Grandma and I all went early. It was one of the first times that I was permitted to go to a party that lasted so far into the night, so I felt very grown up and important. Just about the first thing that I did was to dump my plate of chocolate ice cream into my lap and thereby dampen, not only myself, but the spirits of the rest of the family, as well. I suppose ice cream was made differently in those days or else printed fabrics were less fast, because the stain resisted all of Mother's efforts to remove it the next day. Then a neighbor suggested that she use a little lime in the water. She did and the stain disappeared like magic—but so did my pretty flower baskets.

Another dress that I remember was my Sunday best one. It was made from raw china silk and the material came direct from China to me. A neighbor, Captain MacKenzie, brought it from the Orient as a special gift.

Why a sea captain should ever live in a place so remote from the ocean as Denver did not seem at all strange to us at the time. He would fuss and bother over his garden of turnips and carrots as carefully as if he were growing rare orchids, then suddenly disappear for months at a time while his garden would do just as well without him. During his absence, his wife lived as quietly as a mouse. Indeed, she was almost as invisible when he was around.

Then, with no warning except his shout as he came up the walk from the street, he would appear laden with weird things from some far place. We loved to listen to his stories, for he mentioned Singapore and Naples and Tasmania and talked of cargoes of jute, copra, rum and mahogany as casually as we referred to the candy store at the corner.

Captain MacKenzie was a huge and jolly man with the rumbling voice of a giant. He battled and won over the storms in the Atlantic, typhoons in the Pacific, and told of buffeting his painfully slow way around the Great Horn while tormented seas tried their best to founder his ship.

One day he died in his bed of no particular thing. He just slipped away.

UNCLE SAM

My mother's brother, my Uncle Sam, died no such peaceful death as Captain MacKenzie. His was the lingering death from tuberculosis—although at that time it was more popularly known as consumption. And he almost broke Grandma's heart. First, because he would not become a farmer; later, because he steadfastly refused to conform to her interpretation of a "good, sensible business man."

His jobs were many and varied, usually of short duration. But the one that he liked best and kept the longest was the work around the Tabor Opera House.[3] The name "opera house" is not to be taken too literally, my dears. Although some opera companies did play there, the usual fare was more likely to be week-long stock companies headed by such forgotten stars as Helen Grace, Kirk Bellew and Clifton Mallory. Or one-night stands with Edde Foy, William Faversham and Pavlowa the dancer. Or perhaps The Black Crook, where some of the husbands around town attended the performance incognito and the ladies on the stage wore black tights.

Grandma hated the theatre with a fanatical intensity because she did not understand it. She maintained that the stage was an unspeakable abomination and the players were direct descendents of the devil.

Sam never was happier than when he was called upon suddenly to play a part for one of the numerous road companies. He was considered to be a "quick study"—once, in an emergency, he learned a formidable part and portrayed the character perfectly, when all the time he had for studying the part was the time it took him to walk from our house to the theatre.

To add to Grandma's distress, his services were often required to replace an actor who was too drunk to perform, although sometimes it was because the performer had got "gold fever" and quit the show without notice.

Finally, Sam married an actress and left Denver with a troupe of players. The subject was strictly forbidden at home, but I believe that Uncle Sam was moderately successful as an actor. His marriage was not a happy one, however, and my recollection is that his wife was a suicide. Sam's

---

3. The Tabor Opera House was located in Leadville, a silver mining town that was the second most populous city in Colorado in the late 19th century, after Denver, which was 100 miles to the east. It hosted Oscar Wilde in 1882.

health was broken when he returned home and he died soon after. Although she was grief-stricken, Grandma considered his death to be a just punishment for his sins.

ADVENTURES WITH LAURA

After glancing at the last few pages I fear that I have given you the impression that I spent most of my younger life climbing fences, fighting and being the tom-boy generally, and that is not true. As a matter of fact, my two obsessions were my music and my sister. She was intensely fond of me, and I, of her.

Laura Pearl should have grown up to be an evangelist or a Samaritan. She was, both by nature and desire, deeply religious and she became more devout as she grew older. She knew her bible thoroughly and she read it with great understanding. She had a compassion for the actions of others that I never could approach.

Do not conclude that she was not a normal girl though. Her thrill was no less than mine whenever she would show me the blood-stained handkerchief—the memento from the night of the Chinese massacre in Denver, before I was born.[4]

That night when the citizens started to rid the city of Chinese by killing them—and they did a most thorough job of it, too—but which ended with a battle between the anti- and the pro-Chinese whites. Mother, in town on business, was caught in the midst of the fighting with her five-year-old baby and with me about to be born.

Mother dropped to the pavement with her body covering my sister, until a man hoisted both of them to his shoulder and carried them into the lobby of the Albany Hotel. Neither of them were injured seriously but with that handkerchief in my hand I could visualize them bleeding from every pore.

Laura likewise was as deliciously terrified as I when Grandma decided to send us to Chicago alone as her agents in an oil property transaction.

---

4. October 31, 1880.

Grandma dreaded riding in trains—the motion of the cars often made her violently ill. Further, she had decided that it was time for Laura and me to gain some business experience.

"Grace, you are a big girl now, practically a young lady"—I was fourteen[5]—"and Laura, you have a methodical mind. I want you to go to this address in Chicago and ask for this gentleman. Do not talk with anyone else either in the office building or on the street. This gentleman is the representative of the Standard Oil Company and I have written him that you will come."

Then she pinned duplicate written instructions and directions inside each our blouses and took us to the station. She told us that we were to agree on a decision about the property after we talked with the man and that she would be satisfied with our decision.

We traveled by day coach and slept in our clothing on those uncomfortable, plush covered seats, because sleepers were apt to be dens of iniquity—second only to opium orgies. And we lunched from our paper bags of food, for in a diner a girl might be tempted to "trade her soul" in exchange for a steak dinner and a pot of doped coffee. In fairness, let me say that there was some basis for Grandma's qualms. White slavery was a national problem at that time and girls were being shanghaied with regularity.

When we reached Chicago we sat on a long bench in the station while we dragged forth our instructions and rehearsed our speeches. Grandma had written down our route from the station to the office building, but she had drilled us so thoroughly that we did not have to refer to it.

We were to walk, of course; taxi riding was vulgar. We were both too impressed with the importance of our errand to enjoy the shop windows as we went uptown. That was a pleasure we were saving for the return trip. But when we went back to the station, our feet were so sore and our ankles so tired from the rough, cobblestone pavements that nothing could have enticed us to stop along the way.

Our man was wonderful. His deep, brown eyes twinkled at our youthfulness and our serious expressions, but he was horrified to learn that we had walked all the way from the station. He insisted that we rest before he would talk with us.

---

5. 1898.

I told him exactly what Grandma had said regarding the property and that she would abide by our decision. To be sure, that was not the way we had rehearsed it, but the original speech did not fit the occasion at all.

Laura said she thought we should sell if the price was right. (Grandma had given a selling figure but told us to keep it a secret in case we decided to sell—at least not to divulge it until after our man made his offer, which might be higher.)

Then he asked me if I agreed with my sister. I said "no"—that I was of the opinion that we should lease the land to the Standard Oil Company because then Grandma would be assured of an income.

"I am sure that you are both most sincere young ladies," he said, "but I agree with you, Grace. Your property is in the center of a proven field and by means of a lease your grandmother will receive a substantial income for a long time."

Laura and I whispered together and then told him that we had both decided on the lease arrangement.

The conference over, our man wanted to take us to lunch which we refused so vehemently that he had difficulty keeping a smile from his face. He offered to send us back to the station in a taxi which we also refused, to his chagrin.

When we gave Grandma the papers granting the lease, she told us how proud she was that we had come to the right conclusion. To be truthful, I wanted to make a small point of the dutiful but painful walk back to the station in spite of the proffered taxi, but Laura advised against it. She always knew the diplomatic thing to do; reluctantly, I agreed.

Pearl was a self-taught cornetist of ability, although she would play only for religious occasions; never being particular whether it was a solemn church affair or with a Salvation Army band on a street corner.

I recall that once she got me to sing with such a group, she accompanying on her horn. We practiced together for a long time and for a week or more we were quite successful. I loved it. But one evening Mother passed by just as I finished a solo. A man, also passing just ahead of her called out, "Go to it, sister. You're the best looking gal I've seen on this corner in a long time."

Then he laughed and flipped a silver dollar onto the bass drum and continued on down the street. Never a word about the song or the excellent music.

That finished me with the Salvation Army. I sang solo parts in the various churches and at church gatherings and that was all right with Mother, but ever after she had a questionable opinion of the Salvation Army. She contributed willingly and regularly to them but I could have no further part in either their entertainments or their concerts.

Chapter Four

Chicago

When I was about sixteen years old,[1] Professor Ciaffano told Mother that further lessons with him were a waste of valuable time; that I had absorbed all that he could do for me. He advised her to send me to New York or Chicago for advanced instruction. He reluctantly concluded that, in spite of his original opinions, I would become a concert singer.

It was not until after I reached Chicago and had the opinion of other voice instructors that I realized that the good man did have hopes for me from the beginning but he disparaged my chances of success to insure my most complete application. He probably prayed that the proper physical proportions would develop in due time. If only he knew!

Figure 4.1.   Grace as a young woman

Once Mother had made the decision to send me to Chicago, there was little delay in completing the arrangements. She took me to the city (this

---

1. 1900.

time we went by Pullman), engaged an instructor and located quarters for the fall of that year.

But I was not to go alone. That was unthinkable. Mother insisted that she could not leave Grandma and Laura, so I was to have a companion. And not just any old companion. The specifications were most exacting. She must be middle-aged, with an unassailable background; she must be of a minatory[2] manner and qualified to serve as a combination guardian, housekeeper and preceptress.

This, I thought, was going to cause a long delay, for surely no one being could possibly possess all of these qualities to a sufficient degree. But Mother located her without apparent difficulty and as soon as the summer was over I was off with Miss Crandall, a New England spinster. Miss Crandall had come to Denver as mentor to a girl from Boston, who had weak lungs. The altitude was beneficial. She had recovered completely and had married a mine owner from Leadville.

Mother had chosen wisely, for Miss Crandall (her first name was Sofia) took her responsibilities seriously to the extreme. She was adamant about my diet, my clothes, my practicing; and each morning before my voice lesson, she tutored me in a number of uninteresting subjects.

There was nothing the matter with my lungs, nevertheless she tried her best to interest me in a daily dose of raw egg in milk and, of all things, an afternoon nap! With all of Chicago to be explored!

And how she counseled me about my friends, for I utilized the time she wanted me to waste napping to acquire a good many. It was Miss Crandall's firm conviction that, having chosen to pursue a career, I should do so without the distraction of much entertainment. A lively game of whist in the parlor in the evening, followed by a bed-time cup of hot chocolate, was her idea of a gay evening and one worthy of discussion at breakfast next morning. You will understand that that was her conviction, not mine.

Mother understood that I would have friends, but she wanted to be sure that they were the right sort and she insisted on a chaperone at all times. Grandma was more broadminded. Mother visited us with regularity and Grandma came along whenever she felt that she could endure the trip. In fact, it seemed uncanny how their trips to Chicago so often coincided with my interest in a new man. I began to suspect that Miss Crandall was not so easily fooled as I had imagined.

---

2. Menacing, threatening.

SUITORS

One man whom I was becoming a trifle serious toward and who was obviously becoming more serious over me was Bruce Harrington. Bruce was a marvelous companion and I did so enjoy being with him. He sent flowers almost every day, and he even pretended that he was happy to have Miss Crandall accompany us. Although we did manage quite well without her whenever it could be managed. But Bruce was a manufacturer of embalming fluids and disinfecting soaps such as are used in public washrooms. Mother and Grandma both ridiculed his business to the point where I dropped the poor man in desperation.

Another beau was Ralph Slocum who was the only son in a wealthy family near Chicago. Ralph wanted me to marry him—his ring was magnificent. But we were to live in India from which country his father imported rare fabrics and tapestries. Ralph was to assume the managership of the exporting end of the business and to superintend purchases. Most fortunately, I was unable to overcome the family objections to that affair, for Ralph contracted a malignant fever and died during his first months abroad. He had not married.

Still another serious suitor was John Barber and he was a banker. I wore his ring for a short time. It was the most conservative one so far. In fact, it was tiny. John was a careful man with a dollar. We used a street car instead of a taxi quite often and we dined at his home far oftener than elsewhere. A carefully worded note honored many occasions instead of flowers. Certainly I was not looking for a man that spent all of his money. But neither was I content with one who saved it so lovingly.

When I became engaged to your father, I returned three rings in one evening, which should constitute a record of some kind or other.

CHARLES MATHER-SMITH

All my life, the most innocuous happenings have had the most profound effect.

Doctor McNeil, back in Denver, was a family friend for many years. So the doctor, imagining me a stranger in a strange city and therefore probably badly in need of company, sent me a letter of introduction to a cousin of his with the suggestion that, should I ever find myself in that neighborhood, I might like to call. He did not know, of course, that the address was just around the corner from our rooms.

That is how I met Mr. Charles Mather-Smith,[3] the father of the man that I was to marry. I liked Mr. Mather-Smith immediately and he was so gracious and kind that even Miss Crandall approved. He was a widower[4] and lived in a fine old mansion that still is a landmark in Chicago.[5] He talked so enchantingly about his many exquisite heirlooms that I was entranced.

His wife had been Sarah Emilie Rozet, a direct descendant of Jean Roset, the famous Frenchman who forsook the acclaim of his own country and came to America before the Revolution.[6] He became an intimate friend and confidant of George Washington. Many pieces of furniture, the silver and a fine old clock brought from France by Jean were among the treasures then in the Mather-Smith home. Some of these same things, including the clock, are now a part of my collection of antiques.

Mr. Mather-Smith himself was a descendant from Cotton Mather of pre-Revolutionary fame. Cotton Mather traced his ancestry back to Egbert, the first Saxon king of all England in the sixth century.[7]

Mr. Mather-Smith asked me to accompany him during his afternoon drive the next day. Certainly I accepted although, strangely enough, Miss Crandall did not. Each afternoon he drove around the park if the weather was fine—or rather, his coachman drove, for Mr. Mather-Smith's eyes were very bad—and each afternoon he begged me to be his companion. Naturally I was thrilled, so I managed it as often as I could. And I made the most of those drives. The smart afternoon costume of that time was light colored linen. To my escort's delight, I wore an assortment of tailored linen suits, sometimes white, often pink or blue. And always a large picture hat, plus a ruffled parasol to match my suit.

---

3. According to his daughter Ann, it was Charles Mather Smith's son Charles Frederic Mather Smith who started to hyphenate his name in the 1900s so that he would no longer receive mail addressed to his neighbor in Highland Park, Illinois, J.P. Smith.

4. His wife Sarah Emily (or Emilie) Rozet Smith died on March 26, 1903.

5. At 12 Walton Place.

6. See the Appendix about the Mather-Smith Family for more information about the Rozets.

7. See the Appendix about the Mather-Smith Family. In a letter to Grace Mary Turner dated February 10, 1965, Richard S. Bull, Jr. (Fred's grandson, then President of the family business, Bradner Smith & Company, who was known for his sense of humor) characterized this claim of descent from King Egbert as "getting into the realm of sheer balderdash. In fact, the odor of hokum begins to arise from the genealogy with almost overpowering strength around 1800."

Mr. Mather-Smith had taken his daily airings alone for so long that when he began to appear with a companion so frequently, it caused some comment. The day that one of the society columns mentioned it, identifying me not by name, but as "the most beautiful woman on the boulevard," I was enthralled. Mr. Mather-Smith, however, did not seem to think it at all momentous. "Of course you are, my dear," he said, "I decided that the first time we met. Surely you do not imagine others less observant than I?" That was one of the few moments in my life when I have been truly embarrassed.

Mr. Mather-Smith loved the opera but he could no longer enjoy going because of his eyes, but he liked nothing better than to discuss themes and stars whenever I dined at his home. He was always jolly—I cannot remember ever seeing him otherwise. And he had a priceless sense of humor of a delicate kind together with an unbounded capacity for indulging himself in its interpretation.

When Carmen, with Madame Bériza,[8] the great Metropolitan Opera and Parisian star and who was my princess of shining perfection, was announced as coming to Chicago, we talked about it for hours.

On the evening before the opening performance, Mr. Mather-Smith invited me to go with him. He said he should like to hear the score once more even if he could not see the performers.

Madame Bériza was magnificent and I remarked that nothing could please me more than to meet her. Mr. Mather-Smith reminded me that the company would be in the city for the entire week and that maybe he could locate someone who could arrange it. In the meantime, he was in a mood to break all of the rules this night, so would I care to have a bite to eat at a restaurant across the street? I certainly would. In the restaurant he asked me to wait while he called his home to instruct his driver about calling for us. He took a long, long time and when he did appear it was to inform me that he had engaged a private room for our supper.

With no suspicion or warning, I walked into the dining room to face the entire cast from Carmen, including my star. He had arranged all of it beforehand and his fake telephone call was to enable the company to assemble before I came in. And not Madame Bériza but I, was the guest of honor.

---

8. Marguerite Bériza (born 1880; died sometime after 1930) was a French soprano who performed extensively in the United States.

I was entranced, terrified and speechless. My memory of that evening is one happy, noisy blur. I do not remember meeting my idol. I am sure that I did but I am equally sure that I never uttered one intelligent word to her.

Years later I again met this grand lady under circumstances which were entirely different and when I felt not the slightest nervousness. Only elation and gratitude. That event comes later in this story.

Mr. Mather-Smith always was delighted to hear from his son, Frederic. Frederic was in Baden-Aheim for treatment of a heart condition. His letters told of his continued improvement and, although I had never seen him, each cheering letter was an occasion which we celebrated at his home for dinner while Mr. Mather-Smith read the letter aloud. These celebrations were especially enjoyable whenever my host's daughter, Mary Rozet, could join us.

MARY ROZET SMITH

Mary Rozet was tall, fair and quite shy. She was the most serious and at the same time the most vivacious lady I have ever known. Her life was completely dedicated to the success of Hull-House, the first settlement house in Chicago; and to her dearest friend Jane Addams, the lady who had conceived and who operated Hull-House. It is questionable whether Hull-House could have survived its early financial difficulties had it not been for the whole-hearted aid of Mary Rozet. When her own considerable resources were not adequate she successfully appealed to her friends and to her father. Mr. Mather-Smith was most generous in response. For forty-three years—until her death[9]—Mary Rozet's life was absorbed in the progress of Hull-House, although she did find time for activities in other national and civic organizations whose goals lay parallel to those of Hull-House.

In spite of these exhausting activities, she never neglected her family to the slightest degree. She was devoted to her father and she made the most of his narrowing activities. Toward the end of his life when he became

---

9. Mary Rozet Smith was born on December 23, 1868, and died on February 22, 1934.

blind, she spent hours with her father, being gay and witty although she was grief-stricken.[10]

CHARLES FREDERIC MATHER-SMITH

From Mary Rozet and Mr. Mather-Smith I learned that Frederic[11] had been divorced recently after an unfortunate marriage and that his heart disorder was the result of that ordeal.[12] His recovery was now almost complete and he planned to be home within a month.

In those early 1900's, a divorce was still considered as a mild social blemish. A divorced man was not actually an outcast of course, but it was somewhat difficult for him to find himself in the unescorted company of unmarried ladies. The girls, under parental admonishment, preferred to meet such men in mixed gatherings only. It was a ridiculous convention, with the

Figure 4.2.   Charles Frederic Mather-Smith

ladies adhering to it on one hand and the men blithely ignoring it on the other. So far, in this world, I know of no rules which successfully control the dictates of love.

For when Frederic returned and I met him, I knew at once that he was the man I would marry. All of the formal barriers and most of the rules of society were swept aside as soon as it was evident that he likewise was

10. Charles Mather Smith died on June 16, 1912.
11. Charles Frederic Mather Smith was born in Chicago on November 21, 1863.
12. He also had a daughter from his first marriage named Sarah Rozet (known as "Sally"), who later married Richard S. Bull, who became President of the family business, Bradner Smith & Company, after Fred retired in 1929.

attracted to me. A perfect example of love at first sight. The fact that he was older than I by almost twenty years was of no significance whatever. In Fred I found all of the qualities of his father magnified, plus a charm of his own that became continuously more engaging as long as we were together.

Mother, as was to be expected from one who firmly believed that all social conventions must always be obeyed and never flaunted, was horrified. As soon as she was convinced that here was an affair which was more than serious, she came on to Chicago with Grandma as an additional line of defense and took an apartment in the neighborhood. She moved me in with her and discharged Miss Crandall, not for any neglect of duty but rather because this situation required special and delicate handling.

She tried so nobly to dissuade me with an amplified version of her successful campaign against Bruce. Repeatedly, she reminded me of the difference in our ages and of the possible consequences therefrom. Fred's former marriage was another big count against him. She usually referred to him as "your second-hand man."

In my own mind, I was so sure, that all of her arguments were wasted time and effort.

Grandma, on the other hand, was sure I was choosing wisely. She, you will remember, had married David when he was twice her age and nothing but happiness had resulted for both of them. She could not foresee, quite naturally, that I was to pioneer almost as primitively as she had, or she would have presented hours of argument in favor of the more mature and established husband under such circumstances.

Fred, in spite of Mother's ladylike frigidity, was always most gracious to her and never indicated by words or actions, that he knew she was giving him a rough time of it.

He thought Grandma was a wonder. He was genuinely interested in progressive American history and he would talk with her for hours about her early experiences. He was especially curious about grandfather David and his rise in the world against such obstacles. Likewise, he never tired of hearing more about the journey across the Plains. Some of my memorabilia concerning Grandma's early life are the result of listening to those sessions.

Mother never was wholly convinced of Fred's complete devotion to me until she witnessed his distracted concern for my well-being when Grace Mary was on the way to becoming our first child.

WEDDING DAY AND BIRTHDAY

We were married, as I have said, on the 28th day of May in 1908.[13] Our marriage in Chicago undoubtedly would have been a successful affair because of the Mather-Smiths' social standing, in spite of Fred's recent divorce from another prominent family. But rather than strain the position of the family, we preferred to journey to Detroit where Father had a close friend, the rector of the Episcopal Church in that city, who was most happy to unite us.

It was when we were arranging for the wedding license that, for the first time in my life, I had occasion to swear to my exact age. I gave it as twenty-three although I never have known precisely when I was born.

It was vanity of Mother's, who had a most youthful face and figure, to prefer to be known as Laura's sister instead of her mother when we were travelling. Accordingly, she had destroyed every known reference to my birth date. To make the confusion perfect, there is no official record on file. Some people have understood that Mother, Sister and I were all off-spring of Grandma's. And when it is put exactly that way, I do not believe there is a fib involved, although some of us are off-spring once removed.

At any rate I have accepted the date of 1884 as being correct although it is the least flattering of three that are offered. My cousin, Mrs. Dillard Beck, who is still living, insists that I was born in 1889 and she convincingly links my birth with other events of that year. Also, among some family papers, I have come across one in a hand writing which I cannot identify, which indicates that I was born in 1890. All of which seems of small consequence now.[14]

The calendar chronicling of the number of years one has lived always has seemed to me to be an archaic inheritance of our civilization anyway. Some future generation may choose to calculate age by the condition of the mind rather than by the mathematical age of the bones which encase it.

---

13. As stated once before, Grace was actually married on June 27, 1908.

14. One suspects that the lady doth protest too much and that the vanity of the mother was passed on to the daughter. Indeed, throughout her memoir Grace cites an astonishing number of men who felt compelled to declare their admiration for her appearance, which of course embarrassed her mightily.

Chapter Five

Pioneering in Oakland

I have told you how we were side-tracked from our original honeymoon plans in New York and how we eventually found ourselves as pioneers in the interior of Florida instead. But I did not remind you that my trousseau, chosen to luxuriate in Europe—my trunks of beautiful frocks, my suits and gowns, my shoes, slippers and underthings were destined instead (with the exception of the underthings) to awe and, I presume, to shock the natives here in the backwoods.

Fortunately for both of us, a good part of my hated, but nevertheless learned, tutelage in housekeeping had been thorough. I surely needed it now. It was I who prayed, beat and cajoled the wood stove into submission, often in tears because of its cussedness. By rapid degrees I learned to produce an edible end result from the collection of utterly strange vegetables, fish and wild game. And in between times I tried to keep some order of cleanliness about the place while the carpenters, stone masons, roofers and painters tried their best to see that it never was orderly. It was just as well that Father had his gun with him the day that the plumber dropped his bucket of red lead right in the center of my freshly scrubbed kitchen floor.

Figure 5.1. Entrance to Edgegrove Farms

We built a central chimney enormous enough to provide fireplaces for all of the rooms that faced it. There were hearths in the living room, the room that is now the library and one in each of the bedrooms upstairs. To the natives, it was one of the wonders of the state. They could not understand why anyone should require that much heat—especially in Florida. Actually, they were envisioning the labor of supplying it with wood, for those fires ate wood almost as fast as a forest fire.

Father got Negroes to clear away the tangle surrounding the house and to make a wide pathway to the lake. Later we bordered the path with the twin rows of palms that are there today. We had some of our furniture and hangings shipped down from the north and we travelled over the rough sand roads to Orlando for the rest of them. That road was nothing more than a meandering path through the woods when we first used it. Because it wandered to stay on solid ground between the swamps, it was five or six miles longer than the road to Orlando now.

Father bought one of the first Buick automobiles, together with a huge supply of extra parts. It was a touring car of course, with all polished brass trimmings and with a single rumble seat at the rear.

Figure 5.2.   Twin rows of palm trees leading from the house at Edgegrove Farms down to Lake Apopka

I am sure that we sported the first linen dusters, goggles and motoring caps in the state. Also, I believe that I was the first woman to drive an automobile in Florida. This certainly caused much whispered comment among the not yet emancipated women of Oakland as well as some outspoken resentment from the men. To the natives, "it wasn't proper to go gallivantin' around like that."

The resentment did not last for very long because every time I went anywhere in the car I took a full load of neighbors along with me. There was one other automobile in Oakland at that time but its owners never gave anyone a ride, regardless of the circumstances.

Each evening I drove into Winter Garden for our milk, loaded and packed with all the children we could cram in the car. We drove to the home of the elder George Smith and there in his orchard he would stalk one of his cows and milk our pails full. Who ever dreamed of germs, undulant fever or pasteurizing in those days?

We never left for Orlando without taking extra jacks, chains, rope, a shovel or two, a plank and assorted spare parts for the emergency certain to occur somewhere along the way. If we pulled to one side of the road to permit a wagon to pass, the car would sink into the soft sand without fail.

I always carried a .22 rifle along to drive the cows from the right-of-way. They paid no attention whatever to our shouts and evinced only a friendly interest in our horn. In fact, I believed that they got onto the road whenever they heard the car, so that they could enjoy the inevitable blasts from the klaxon. The noise from the rifle had more effect though, and a little dust kicked up between their front legs always would do the trick. We were very careful never to injure a cow or steer. First, there was the humanitarian reason. Also, one could not determine whether the animal was a single cow owned by a farmer in the neighborhood or whether it was a stray from one of the large herds farther south. Wanton or accidental injury to any of that stock could result in plenty of trouble. The cattle ranchers were pretty tough customers on occasion.

CATTLE BARONS

It sounds fantastic now to recall that when we moved to Florida there were cattle barons as autocratic as any you will read about in stories of the Old

West. They made the laws for their tremendous ranches and they enforced them with men and guns.

There were cowboys galore and their exploits often were as legendary as those of the characters in the most satisfying western movie. Because of the lack of open country, the cowboys became proficient in the use of a long, short-handled whip, often twenty feet or more in length. With it, a man could stop a steer by flicking the tip of the whip around its neck or legs. Or, with a crack like a pistol shot, snap a piece of flesh from the flank of a recalcitrant animal.[1]

The wealth of these barons was fabulous. The stories one hears about the bags of gold pieces left in plain sight around the house to provide a source of ready cash, are not fiction. Father and I saw such a bag on a hall table in a ranch house and all the evidences were that it was a fixture there.

There were rustlers who were sometimes caught and hung where they stood. There were the traditional gamblers, sharpers and hold-up men. And there were feuds and pitched battles between warring outfits.

It was not uncommon, but always thrilling, to see booted and armed cattlemen talking peacefully in front of the courthouse in Orlando or near Hyatt's livery stable, then located where Yowell and Drew's[2] is today.

While it is not part of my story, I cannot refrain from an expression of regret that poor inbreeding of stock as well as a total lack of official interest in tick and pest control undoubtedly kept Florida from taking a more prominent place as a supplier of beef to the nation at a time when it was easiest to do so.[3]

EXPERIENCES WITH THE BUICK

Before I shunted off into the cattle industry, I was recalling our experiences with the Buick. In one way and another, that car and its successors livened my backwoods life considerably from time to time.

There is the much repeated story of the time I went through Winter Garden in a hurry—I usually was in a rush—and the policeman stopped

1. Some say the loud crack of the Florida cowboy's whip was the origin of the term "Cracker" to describe the early pioneer settlers of Florida.
2. A department store.
3. Cattle ranching, based around Kissimmee, was—and still is—one of Florida's biggest businesses.

Figure 5.3. Grace at the wheel of her Buick. Reproduced courtesy of the Winter Garden Heritage Foundation.

me for speeding. I was going no faster than usual but on this particular day, either he did not feel so good or perhaps there had been complaints.

Being police chief, policeman and also Justice of the Peace enabled him to compress the activities of each job into one package.

"That will cost you just ten dollars for exceeding the speed limit in town, Mrs. Mather-Smith."

I was only going a few miles beyond town and intended to come right back, so I said, "I am coming back in a few minutes, so here is twenty dollars and keep out of my way."

He had the money in his hand and I was far down the road before he realized that he had given me tacit permission to return through town as fast as I pleased. He was a good sport though, so he was conveniently out of sight when I came back. We often laughed about it afterward.

Another time I was late for a party being given by a hostess who expected her guests to be prompt above all things. I was crossing the old iron bridge going into Orlando when another policeman stopped me. But this time, instead of arresting me for speeding—which I was—he was asking for still more speed. His son had been snake-bit and he wanted to get to him. When we reached his home a neighbor had incised the wound and sucked most of the venom out. I took the father, mother and the boy to a doctor, but in the excitement I had forgotten to call my hostess.

That day I was dressed in a pink organdy dress with matching hat, both of which were more than a little soiled when I reached the party. I suppose that I looked like a tramp and the dear, precise lady clearly thought I was acting like one. She never forgave me, nor did she ever invite me again.

On still another occasion I was leaving Orlando for home and had just crossed the bridge when two young men hailed me for a ride. Today that would be a hazardous thing to do, but then we thought nothing of offering a ride to anyone on foot. They were both pleasant young men. When we mired in the sand, they happily dug us out and pushed the car back on the road. They thanked me politely just before we reached Oakland.

Next morning I learned that I had aided in the escape of two desperate criminals, one of whom was described as a "cold-blooded killer." This man had killed a woman who had befriended him with a ride near Jacksonville a few months before. Now he had escaped from prison with another man who was serving twenty years. If they ever were captured, I did not learn of it.

Another day I dressed with particular care for a party being given by Bernadina Hale, and fortunately I arrived a little early. As I left the car I slammed the door behind me and tore a yard or more from the rear of my pretty new dress. I hurried downtown where I discovered that most of the stores had closed for the day. Finally, I located a tiny, cheap little place near the outskirts. With many misgivings I bought a dress for something like two dollars and a half. The one I was discarding had cost seventy. I hurried to the powder room in the hotel, changed and reached the party in good time. So far as I know, no one noticed anything unusual about my costume.

GARDENING, HUNTING AND FISHING

In the fall of the first year we started our garden. We planted every vegetable listed in the catalogue. In the unbelievably rich soil they grew bountifully. Varieties which could be grown only by the experts in the north, grew like weeds. In spite of our continued thinning out the less hardy plants, we were literally knee deep in vegetables that winter. We distributed loads of them among the neighbors and still we could not eat the balance. In some ways, this abundance was wonderful for me. Instead of puzzling over new ways to serve the same old things day after day, I could simply dish up a new one.

Father kept us plentifully supplied with wild game. Turkeys, quail and delicious wild ducks were so plentiful that meat for the table was obtained by the simple process of stepping into the surrounding woods with a gun.

We fished every day and what sport that was! I, who had known nothing at all about fishing since my bent pin and grocer's twine days, learned to cast a plug onto a bonnet with accuracy and to boat my own fish.

I learned to handle a boat like an Indian guide and I could maneuver it to Father's complete satisfaction whenever he was tied onto a big one. And they did run pretty big those days. Many times we brought home a bass that was more than a meal for all of us.

We put out night lines near the house and raising them in the morning was like opening a surprise package. Our lines might hold almost anything that swam or crawled. The idea was, of course, to try for some of the enormous catfish who fed mainly during the night. We caught them in quantity but we also hooked water moccasins, alligators, mudfish, gar, turtles, bream, bass and one time we caught a seagull. The night we caught the otter he took line, anchor and all the other hooked fish with him. We found him later, dead.

Part of our regular equipment in the boat was a rifle to destroy the moccasins which we found in the cypress and oak trees along the water's edge. They would hang suspended from limbs to watch for small fish to pass under them. Once or twice one dropped into our boat as we passed under a tree.

I learned to hit an alligator in his most vulnerable spot—his eye—when they came ashore after our chickens. Rattlesnakes were numerous, especially before we cleared the land and planted the groves. I have killed them, but in all the years I have lived in Florida I never have been seriously threatened by one. Furthermore, I can almost count on the fingers of one hand the number of people whom I know to have been struck by one. Today, I never kill a snake or an animal. I am convinced that they strike or kill only in self defense, as far as humans are concerned, and if not startled or molested, they are not harmful.

NOVELTIES

Father lost no time putting our flowing well to work. He installed a water ram at once and erected a storage tank on the higher ground behind the house. Water under pressure all over the house was a novelty indeed for the natives, but the bathroom was a sensation.

There was not another bathtub in town—in fact, most of the natives never had seen one. So it created more interest than anything we had down so far. Some professed to consider it only as a rich man's luxury and therefore really not practical. Nevertheless, they stopped by time after time just to take another look at it.

But the toilet surely was one of the world's wonders. Only they did not refer to it as a toilet. It was a "syphon jet"—that was the name baked into the enamel. I hate to think of the untold gallons of water that poor ram had to lift only for the demonstrations. Father was in the paper business[4] so we always had unlimited supplies of tissue, but bales and bales of it went down the drain just to prove its flushing properties.

FAIRY AND MAGICIAN

It occurs to me that the children were most entranced by the tub. They, the dears, had known only the inconvenience of bathing each Saturday in the washtub on the kitchen floor or, as was not uncommon, a scrubbing with laundry soap in the lake. They came in droves to smell our soap—sweet soap they called it—and to gaze at the tub. And, wonder of wonders, sometimes to bathe in it. Often I would scrub them until my arms ached and then put them to sleep in rows across the beds.

In the morning, to be sure, they each had to be fed before leaving for school. What times those were! If we had the time I always asked each what she would like for breakfast. They took for granted that "Miss Grace" was something of a fairy with a little magician mixed in, so they never hesitated. It was usually breakfast food and cream. They would put their little ears almost into the bowls to hear the flakes pop as they soft-

---

4. Fred became President and later Chairman of Bradner Smith & Company, the family business. See the discussion of the founding of Bradner Smith & Co. in the Appendix about the Mather-Smith Family.

ened in the cream. Or perhaps it would be soft-boiled eggs and toast. Both of these were luxuries to them. At home it was likely to be grits and gravy. One morning one little girl said that all her life she had wanted liver and bacon for breakfast. She got it, bless her heart.

Sometimes we could not possibly get them all ready for both breakfast and school. By then, we had a chauffeur and it was his responsibility to get them to school without being tardy. He would halt his load at Brock's grocery for bags of cookies and whatever else could be eaten on the run. Then off for Tildenville, for we had no school in Oakland. Today, with the ordered precision of raising our children, such feeding methods sound terrible, but they thrived on it.

How very many times I think of those children. Each year Father would arrange for a private [railroad] car to bring us to Oakland and another to take us back to Highland Park in the spring. When the switch engine would whistle to clear the crossing and shunt our car onto the siding, there was no need to tell the youngsters whose car it was. It was "Miss Grace" and her family. To them, Father was part of my family.

If we arrived during school hours, a recess was declared while the children came down to the station to greet us. They would stand in rows while our boxes and bags were unloaded, and with hushed voices speculate on the possible contents of each piece.

The joyful parade and the bouquets were not a part of our departure in the spring. They would appear to see us off but now they stood beside the track with sad faces and tearfully waved us out of sight.

I have said that my clothes were unusual for this part of Florida. The girls were hypnotized by them. After dinner they came in droves just to see what I would be wearing that evening. We sat on the porch while they got their fill of a particular costume. Many nights I removed a dress which looked like a towel in a lumber camp from their hands.

One evening Father and I were returning from Orlando with a load of things for the house when we drove into a neighborly feud just developing in good form. One faction was on either side of the road, pot-shotting the other from behind bushes. They showed no inclination to declare a truce to permit us to pass so we speeded up to thirty miles an hour and barged through. If you don't think that is fast driving through loose sand, you should try it some time.

When we got home the youngsters went over every inch of the car hoping to find a bullet hole or two. We were almost sorry we hadn't been hit at least once, just to please them.

Each spring, before we left for the north, came May Day. I cannot recall ever having seen this day celebrated elsewhere in the Florida manner. For weeks in advance, the children, both boys and girls, saved their pennies and their sweets. They coaxed and heckled the station master for quantities of that peculiar yellow copy paper then used by railroads. This they cut into strips and stretched the edges to simulate crepe paper ruffles. Larger pieces were fashioned into rosettes and flowers. All of these went to decorate the May baskets, and into them went the hoard of candies and cookies.

The day was a sort of a combination of Easter with its pretty baskets and Hallowe'en, for the children would come to the house in the evening. One of the boys then hammered on the porch floor with a heavy stick while the rest scrambled for hiding places. Then one little girl stood at the door with the basket.

My part in the proceedings was to pretend to hunt for each one and then invite them all in for orange juice, doughnuts and candy, and an evening of games and fun. After three or four such groups had serenaded us and then joined the group, you can imagine the resulting turmoil. But we loved it and looked forward to May Day each year.

Father built a huge dock over the lake. It had a comfortable bench at the end and a large boathouse. How many romances were sparked on that bench? Only my friend Destiny knows. The boathouse became a junior community center.

As the children grew older it became our dance hall. The girls were eternally trying to raise money for some project or other, so we sold tickets. "Miss Grace" had the only phonograph in town, so that was our orchestra. Usually the dances were well attended but when attendance fell off it was up to me to stimulate it.

One time I went over around Monteverde[5] and invited the boys from there to come and dance with us. They came all right, but at first our girls refused to so much as enter the room with them. They surely were a ferocious looking lot.

---

5. At the southwest corner of Lake Apopka, about seven miles from Oakland.

Figure 5.4. Fred at the wheel of his boat

The girls were dressed in their best frocks while the boys had come over in shirts and overalls. I remember that some of them were barefoot. Their clothes were clean but definitely not what we expected. Nevertheless, they undoubtedly were the best they owned. The timidity soon passed and we enjoyed another successful evening.

The boathouse also served to house our little theatre movement—although we did not call it that. We just gave plays. I never performed in them but I did serve with various girls as director, scene shifter, property provider, advertising manager, make-up artist and business manager. 'Twas I who browbeat the neighbors into buying tickets and then harangued them into coming to the show. It was not enough to buy a ticket, you had to sit through the performance as well.

Dewey Vick was our playwright. We presented melodrama, comedy, westerns and just plain thrillers, with equal facility. And Dewey invented the plots, action and dialogue without apparent effort. I have always contended that she should have developed these talents, for they were considerable.

But Dewey became such a successful business woman, with a sense of civic responsibility which resulted in her becoming Oakland's first and only woman mayor,[6] that I am sure she has no regrets.

GRACE MARY

As I look back from here, I am sure that the first few months of that first year of my marriage were the most tumultuous of my life. When the confusion of finishing the house, clearing the land and planting the garden was at its peak, we learned that I was going to have a child.

Father became possessed. He immediately started to plan an addition to the house for the help he was sure would be required and I think he would have telegraphed north for a governess that first night, had he been left to do as he pleased.

He wanted me to stop fishing, which I did not do, and he cautioned me constantly about straining myself. He sent for Mother, asking her to drop everything and come at once. She came as soon as she could arrange her own affairs although she was most emphatic that no house ever built was large enough for two families.

Father loaded the house with every aid and convenience from safety pins to a teething ring. He had a telephone line run all the way from Orlando at our expense, the first phone in town.

The telephone, incidentally, started a fresh pilgrimage to the house. The children, and some of the grown-ups also, would sit around for hours hoping to hear it ring. They would talk for days in unbelieving wonder after we had been connected with friends in Chicago.

Father engaged a nurse who, for safety's sake, was installed a month in advance. We were prepared for a siege instead of a natural event.

With all of these pre-arrangements the coming of the baby should have been a simple affair, and in reality it was. Simple for everyone but me. Father and I were fishing when the first labor pain occurred. He rushed me to shore and called the doctor in Orlando. Fortunately, the telephone was working—sometimes it went dead at unexpected times—and he arrived promptly. Then all progress ceased.

---

6. Dewey Vick Mathews was mayor of Oakland between 1941 and 1947.

It seemed as if the labor pains never would increase. They stayed at almost the exact timing, but with an intensity just short of excruciating, for endless hours—for so long, in fact, that everyone except Father gradually lost interest in me. Dr. McCuen talked about going fishing for a half day or so, as long as he had to hang around anyway. The nurse sat placidly in a corner with a book before her eyes, entirely oblivious of the fact that I was dying. Even Mother got a little bored and started to look at me with reproach. At last, just when I decided that no human being ever could stand such misery for another minute, Grace Mary decided to join our party.[7] Father had been wishing for a boy, but he cancelled that wish as soon as he saw his daughter.

Even if Father had not kept repeating that I was the greatest woman in the whole wide world, I knew it anyway. I had my first BABY! Now I was going to devote my life to protecting her from sorrow and shielding her from pain.

The next morning the nurse was preparing a cup of coffee in the kitchen, with the baby in her arms, and she dumped the scalding coffee all over my precious baby's side. I had failed in my resolve within the first twenty-four hours.

Nevertheless I was obsessed with her safety. I prayed to God to let me stay awake all night so that I might watch to make sure nothing happened to my treasure. When I handled her, no miser ever gloated more than I. Each afternoon I put her on the porch in her carriage to nap. Then I sat in the window as alert as a robin to watch her every breath.

One evening when we were alone in the house, Grace Mary and I, a wild cat came foraging. I can't think of anything more fearsome that the snarl and cry of a wild cat at night. And this one was a master at curdling one's blood. I put out all the oil lamps and stood in the center of the kitchen floor with my blissfully sleeping darling in my arms and prayed and prayed that he would not get in and harm her. It did not occur to me to wonder if it might be me he was after.

As a matter of fact, he was not after either of us. He was simply infuriated because Father had penned up the chickens and ducks so that he could not get at his usual evening meal.

---

7. Grace Mary was born on April 8, 1909.

The Negro laundress who came next morning, and who had all of the superstitiousness of her race, told me solemnly, "Them catamounts can always smell a new baby."

For a long time I sat in the window with a rifle beside me whenever Grace Mary was on the porch. Now that sounds pretty silly, doesn't it?

You can imagine the novelty Grace Mary was for the children. The town was full of babies of all ages. Most of the girls had younger brothers or sisters, but Grace Mary was something special. She was "Miss Grace's" baby. They might lug their own sisters around like little sacks of potatoes but I never had to caution them against touching the baby. They stood and gazed at her with their hands held tightly behind their backs. They considered it a privilege to sit beside her while she slept outdoors, arguing in whispers as to whose turn it was to keep the insects away with a palm frond fan. Then they took turns wheeling her about when she awakened.

Father was passionately fond of all of you but I think Grace Mary was his favorite. She was first so she had the longest time to work into his heart, so she had a slight advantage over the rest of you. And don't imagine for a minute that she ever failed to capitalize his fondness to her advantage whenever it served her purpose.

When she was quite small I ordered her to bed without her lunch in just punishment for some long forgotten misbehavior. But, as was to be expected, she talked Father into smuggling in a jar of her favorite candy— lemon ball—to replace the lost lunch.

I knew Father better than she, so I located the jar just before Father and I left for a call in the neighborhood. I permitted her to keep the jar, but as an added punishment for trying to put one over on me, I carefully counted the pieces—there were thirty—and explained with gestures, exactly what she might expect if they were not all there when I returned.

Sure enough, when I got home, Grace Mary was still in bed and she had all of the candies. But all thirty of them could have been placed in a pea pod. Each one had been sucked until it was no larger than a match head. Of course I did not punish her. I had stipulated quantity and not size.

Father did not agree with my opinion, about this time, that she was getting just a little too smart for her age. He was sure that it was only a manifestation of her originality. Just as he was confident she would be the wit of the family the morning she first discovered the difference between the chickens and the turkeys.

"Pappala," she cried as she burst in the back door, "I know this is Sunday because all the chickens have their red neckties on."

REBECCA ANN

Grandma also was another one who idolized Grace Mary, although she knew her only as an infant. Grandma hurried south to see this newest member of the family and the first one in so long. She became her slave at sight.

The baby's birth was not the only reason Grandma came to Florida. She was suffering from an advanced case of shingles as well as an intestinal disorder and she hoped that the warm climate might benefit her.

She bought a home just back of us toward the post office, and immediately started to develop a new circle of friends. Grandma never did classify the social status of her friends. She was equally happy with a farmer, seamstress, banker or banker's wife. Her male friends particularly—and she had a good many—insisted that she was the brightest woman in the state. In reality, it is doubtful whether she ever spoke a dozen words an hour to any of them. It was her belief that no man is ever so happy as when he is talking about himself, so she just prodded them along and then sat back to listen.

We were forbidden by Grandma to mention her shingles to any one. She suffered with them constantly. She always wore white china silk things above her waist. Her two-fingered plucking at her blouse was, in reality, an effort to relieve some of the discomfort of her garments' contact with the most painful areas.

Constant expert medical attention did partially improve the shingles but she did not respond to treatment for her abdominal ailment. She died from a blocked intestinal tract when Grace Mary was about a year old.[8]

Although Grandma had a long and full life, one cannot but speculate whether she might not have been with us longer had she been less adamant about her religious and moral beliefs. It is quite unlikely that she ever permitted a complete examination of her body. At her death, one of her two last requests was that she be prepared for burial without disrobing

8. So she died around 1910.

her. Accordingly, the mortician completed his task, working through her arms only. Eight years later when Mother died, this same man, remembering, prepared her body by this same procedure.

Grandma's second request was that she be buried in Chicago. That was accomplished most magnificently by the Order of Masons. David had been a Mason and Grandma numbered many of them among her friends. At her death, they took complete charge of all the necessary duties in Florida and then, at their own expense, removed her body to Chicago and conducted the services there. She is buried in the family plot in Chicago.[9]

BACK TO CHICAGO

Regardless of our wishes, we had to leave early that year. Father's Chicago business and his investments demanded his attention without further delay, while for me there was a tremendous list of things to be taken care of before fall. And for both of us, a formidable back-log of social obligations.

It was after one of these affairs, a party at Mrs. Metzgar's home, that Father decided to perpetrate one of the whimsical surprises of which he was so fond.

The evening was perfect and the distance short so we decided to walk home and window-shop along the way. As we passed Stevens' Brothers store[10] I exclaimed over the huge display of nightgowns that completely filled one window. You all know my weakness for fancy nightgowns, so you can appreciate my delight. They were all beautiful although many of them were intended for occasions much more intimate than regular night wear. I told Father that if I had one of those, I should feel like a "kept woman." He asked me which one I liked best. I never could have picked a favorite from that array and I told him so.

The next morning our living room was practically inundated with boxes and bags from Stevens'. Father had purchased the entire display.

"All I request is that you give none of them away. You must wear each one," was his laughing remark when he came home.

---

9. She is buried in Oak Woods Cemetery on the South Side of Chicago.
10. No doubt the Charles A. Stevens Department Store at 17 North State Street.

I do not remember what became of them all. I presume I wore them to shreds for I know that I kept my promise.

MATHER

During the fall and winter of that year we completed the planting of our first block of citrus trees, started the landscaping in earnest and trimmed the garden down to a one-family size. We finished decorating the house and by spring we had just settled comfortably when it again became necessary to start planning an addition to the house. We now had the news that we were to have another child.

This time the baby was expected near the end of the year. Father decided that the trip south in the fall would be an unnecessary risk so we remained in the north. We located a suitable house in Evanston, in a quiet

Figure 5.5.   Grace Mary and Mather

neighborhood and within commuting distance of Chicago.

My darling Grace Mary had tormented me for an indeterminate time before she could consent to be born. Twenty months later, on December 11th, [1910,] Mather did just the opposite.

I had been working at the sewing machine and had leaned forward to rethread the needle when I felt the first sharp pain. Almost before the doctor arrived, Mather was with us.

This time, I determined, with the entire metropolitan area to choose within, we would find a nurse who would not scald or otherwise damage my baby during his first day on earth. So we engaged a girl who was highly recommended by the doctor. But, we learned belatedly, she had just come off a dithpheria case. Without delay she gave Mather diphtheritic eyes. We despaired of his sight for a few days, but when he started to nurse it cleared up with no lasting effects.

Father was ecstatic. He had a SON! Never have I seen a man so possessed. He paraded the streets in a cutaway coat, top hat, gray gloves and cane. He shouted the news to his friends and told perfect strangers about his new son. He carried an armload of cigars, enough to stock a small cigar store, wherever he went and he passed them out by the handful.

When he was home, he came into the bedroom every few minutes to make sure nothing was going wrong. He began to look for signs of resemblance before the puckery, red wrinkles faded away into human skin. Before Mather had his first meal Father was making tentative plans for his education and then his business career. He was the happiest man in Christendom.

Mather was, as you know, christened Charles Frederic Mather-Smith, a name far too formidable for his young friends. He became Mat to them and Mather to the rest of us.

Mather was a tiny baby when Father came home one morning and asked that I get the baby and Grace Mary ready for a little ride. I protested; it was inconvenient for me and also it was almost noon and we had dinner well under way. But he insisted.

We drove and drove until we reached Highland Park. There, something seemed to go wrong with the car. Father knew nothing about an automobile engine but he raised the hood and puttered away. There was an organ playing in the house we had stopped before. I loved organ music and Father called my attention to it.

Finally he said, "Let's go in and see who is playing that wonderful music."

I thought he had lost his reason for wanting to barge in on a stranger like that.

"I am certain that anyone who plays so beautifully will be complimented at our interest," he said as we went to the door.

I was frightfully embarrassed when we saw the complete dinner on the table until Father said, "This all is yours, my dear—for giving me a son."

That's the kind of man your father was. He had bought and furnished the house, installed the organ, staffed the house and had our first meal all ready before he mentioned a word to me. Father loved to prepare elaborate surprises for me but this was the greatest one of all. I was overcome with joy.[11]

LAURA

Often, our periods of greatest happiness are likely to be tempered with sorrow. Soon after we moved into our new home, Laura,[12] who was with us in Highland Park, consented to remain at home one Sunday morning with Mather so that I might feel at ease regarding him while I sang in church that day.

When we left she was sitting under one of the large trees in the front yard. During our absence she was stricken with a disorder which never was satisfactorily diagnosed. She had Mather in her lap at the time. With her last strength she somehow managed to crawl as far as the house and call the cook to look after the baby. Then she died there on the floor.[13]

---

11. The house was named Matherwood.
12. Grace's older sister Laura Pearl.
13. Laura died in 1912. She had never married.

Chapter Six

Weighty Matters

So many basic ideas have changed during our lifetimes, haven't they?

Today of course the prescription has changed completely, but when Grace Mary was born it was the custom for doctors to order that an expectant mother be fed mightily. "You are eating for two, you know," was the philosophy of it. And the trusting soul would proceed to make things harder for herself by dutifully following instructions.

In my case, I ate and ate, and it showed in added poundage. I imagine one might have filled Lake Apopka with the hot chocolate I consumed before bedtime each night.

According to the misinformed theory of that day, I should have returned to my original weight after the baby was born. But there was something about the aggregate of the fattening foods which started chemical readjustments within me which could not be checked. After Grace Mary was born I had to have all new clothes, even larger than my maternity garments. Long before Ann came along I had increased my weight from the original one hundred and thirty five pounds to an unbelievable and prodigious three hundred and twelve.

Dear old Professor Ciaffano would have been overjoyed at the sight of me.

My friends said that I would lose my husband if I did not do something about my weight. But what? No one seemed to have that answer. No matter how little I ate, every ounce stayed with me. The doctor diagnosed a thyroid condition and prescribed his pills plus gobs of orange juice. Not a pound did I lose.

In desperation I bought some long red flannel underwear and started to do my own washing to melt some of the excess away. My feet got sore,

Figure 6.1.   Grace Mary's second birthday in 1911. Reproduced courtesy of the Winter Garden Heritage Foundation.

my back hurt and every muscle felt like a throbbing tooth. Perspiration ran from me in rivers. But a pound or two was the best I could do.

I tried every diet that was suggested and exercises which left me exhausted and which also left me as stout as before. One friend recommended a salon of specialists who were then enjoying great popularity and I enrolled with them. I was enthusiastic. Certainly, I thought, this treatment was thorough enough to reduce the size of a rock.

First a steam bath where I gasped and panted while my body literally stewed for an hour at a time. Then I was transferred to a torture room for a session in a weird contraption consisting almost entirely of power driven, cast iron rollers. The function of the rollers was to squeeze, pummel and roll the excess away.

There were twelve of those machines in the room and their clanking, thumping and grinding noises, together with the combined groans and squeals of their lady victims, resulted in a fair imitation of Dante's Inferno.

One morning just as my machine got to doing its worst, one of the cast iron rollers broke and poked itself into my stomach. It took some time to attract the attention of the attendants. They were so accustomed to shrieks that they reacted slowly to the real thing, although blood was spurting from the incision. Right then the salon lost eleven other customers.

There was a doctor in the building and he reached me in a matter of minutes. He made a thorough examination and then smiled as he assured me that I was cut only superficially. He said that, fortunately for me, I was so fat that no vital part had been damaged. That time I lost six pounds but it was from fright and not from the treatments.

No matter whether I followed the doctor's orders in the north or dieted and exercised in Florida, the result was always the same. My weight remained at slightly over three hundred pounds.

Then came a time when I had to direct all of my energies in another direction. We were to have another child. The circumstances of Ann's birth should have reduced me by at least fifty pounds, but they did not.

ANN

Although my school mathematics never did include calculus, Father was a good mathematician and surely the doctor could count without resort to his fingers, but between the three of us we managed to miscalculate the birth date by over six weeks. The nurse—again carefully chosen—was a bewildered darling from Pennsylvania and she was with us for almost two months in advance. And again the array of paraphernalia was in readiness.

I had experienced premonitions concerning the birth, one of which was a dream where everyone was frantically searching for a pair of shears at a crucial moment. When I told this to Father, he brought me an enormous pair of paper-hanger's shears as a joke.

On the eventful day Mother suffered a heart attack—a very severe one. The doctor put her to bed with strict instructions regarding her care. Above all things, she was to be protected from shock or worry. Before he left, he examined me and assured me that all was well—that I need not expect my baby for a few days.

Father was then mayor of Oakland[1] and he had to go to an important meeting in town so we were left alone, the nurse and I, with Mother.

---

1. Fred was mayor of Oakland in 1914-15.

Figure 6.2. Grace Mary, Mather and Ann

With no warning that I remember, labor started at about eight o'clock. The nurse tried to reach the doctor by telephone but he had gone over to Apopka on an urgent case and could not be reached.

It is strange how little we learn from experience. This was the third such ordeal for me, but in the emergency I was as helpless as to the procedure as a bride.

Mother must not be alarmed. The nurse became frantic. To be fair, it must be stated that she had been employed to take care of a baby, not to bring one into this world. She cried and wrung her hands until at last she became hysterical.

Because of the pains, I am now ashamed to say that it was with extreme pleasure that I slapped her back to sanity. But that did no good as far as help for me was concerned because now she became dumb. She couldn't think or talk. When last I saw her she was in the center of the living room twisting a handkerchief with her hands. To the best of my knowledge she was there when the doctor came. But he did not come just then.

I searched my brain for any helpful information which might be lurking there. But all that came to me was the recollection that Mother always considered the tea kettle the most sterile thing in the house. I went to the kitchen and discovered that Nanny, our cook, had not left, so between us we got the kettle on the fire. Into it went our ball of string—saved from the packages from Brock's grocery—the shears Father had bought, and a bottle of olive oil.

Once, Mother called to ask what I was doing in the kitchen after she knew I had retired. I do not remember what I told her but it did not alarm her.

I knew it was useless to attempt to send the nurse for Father. Even when she was normal she was terrified in the dark, and I needed Nanny with me.

As for knowledge of what to do, Nanny was as helpless as I, but I knew that, with the placid viewpoint of her race, she would not go to pieces.

Finally, about ten o'clock, Rebecca Ann arrived,[2] with me wondering what on earth had relieved the pains so suddenly. Nanny—bug-eyed— was standing alongside the bed with the steaming tea kettle as per orders.

I would not let her move an inch for several minutes even though she assured me over and over that the baby was here. It did not seem possible that it was all over.

Nanny fished the string out with a fork and I sat up and tied the cord in five places—to make sure. Then came what was the hardest ordeal of my life. There was no pain, of course, but severing that cord was the most terrifying thing I ever attempted. I was so sure it was the wrong thing to do. Then when Ann lay there, still as a doll, I was certain of it.

Nanny timidly suggested that she thought you always held a new baby by the heels and slapped it to start it breathing. So I picked her up and tapped her gently. Nothing happened. Frantically, I hit her hard enough to have knocked her silly. It worked. She started to cry and everything was all right.

We rubbed her with olive oil, wrapped her in blankets and had just settled her by my side when the doctor came.

He found some damage had occurred during delivery—Ann weighed ten and a quarter pounds. It was not until after he fixed me up that he learned the circumstances of her birth.

---

2. Rebecca Ann was born on March 14, 1914.

The nurse distinguished herself once more that evening, by the way. The doctor wanted to administer a little chloroform so he instructed the nurse exactly how to drop the few drops onto a cotton pad placed over my mouth and nose. She dropped them slowly, but into my eye instead of the cotton. I was almost blind for three days afterward.

According to the law of averages, it is reasonable to suppose that I had enough ill-luck by this time. But next evening I started what had all the symptoms of labor pains all over again. So we tried to reach the doctor and again he was in Apopka. The variation was that this time we could contact him. It took him over two hours to get to our house. It had been storming and, fearful that the condition of the roads might delay him, he had crossed Lake Apopka in a small boat in the dark, with only a flashlight to guide him.

He found that proper drainage had not occurred because of my excess weight. The condition was not serious but for more than two weeks I had to lie in bed with piles of bricks under its legs at the top. The discomfort was extreme and whenever I moved, I slid to the foot of the bed. Ann didn't seem to mind any of it. She was contented and I am sure her smile hastened my recovery.

NEW FIGURE

The next year I agreed to sing in a scheduled production of Faust. I wanted to reduce now more than ever. A three hundred pound Margaret was hardly the heroine Goethe had in mind when he wrote the opera.

For weeks, during which time we rehearsed each day, I subsisted largely on lemon juice and crackers. One morning my accompanist and the leading tenor, Octave Dua,[3] came to the house to rehearse and I discovered that I could not sing a note. My voice had left me. With the performance only a week away, we were frantic.

Octave told me of a wonderful Chicago doctor who was most successful keeping singers in voice. Father and I left at once. But we had been given a faulty address so we found our way, not to the famous man, but to the office of his brother.

---

3. Octave Dua (1882-1952) was a Belgian tenor who sang for the Chicago Opera between 1915 and 1922.

This man was practically unknown and certainly unheralded. His office was shabby, he had no receptionist, no nurse and almost no equipment. But he did have a personality. He listened to my story and said he thought he could help me. He scolded me—told me that the main cause of my immediate condition was diet, or rather the lack of it. I had been starving myself. He ordered me home and into bed for three weeks. Furthermore, I was to eat three healthy meals each day. Then he gave me pills and a diet which I was to follow after that time.

That evening he called Father and told him that the pills were only licorice and therefore useless as a reducing agent. He said I had a glandular disorder, unfortunately not uncommon, for which no remedy was known. He added that I seemed happy so he advised against telling me.

The concert was definitely off for me for I stayed in bed and followed his orders completely. After three weeks I started to take his pills by the clock and followed his diet to the letter. It was a simple one. No starches, no sweets, four pills and two glasses of water each day. In spite of constant temptations to do otherwise, I held to my diet and miraculously it started to show its effectiveness.

After the first few days I lost weight at the rate of about four pounds a day. I diminished from a fifty-four inch bust to thirty-six inches in five months. I substituted orange juice to replace my allowance of water with most beneficial results. I experienced no sagging areas in spite of the fast reduction in weight. My doctor told us later that this was the result of the toning action of the citrus juice.

By spring I was back to my original weight, about a hundred and thirty-five. When we got back to Chicago I went to see the doctor again. He definitely did not know me. Still he had no receptionist so he took my data himself.

When I told him my name he said, "How strange. I had another patient with that exact name some time ago. Are you, by chance, a relative?"

It was some time before I could convince him that I was that same patient.

Many of my friends were just as hard to convince. I know I embarrassed some of them, tormenting them before I told them who I was.

The end result of all this was that the doctor became famous almost overnight. When next I saw him he was rolling in money. Those were the days before income taxes and he was acquiring money faster than he could handle it.

I am so happy that I was instrumental in prevailing upon him to settle an ample sum in his wife's name and got him to buy securities to assure his boy's education, for his fortunes warped his self-discipline. He became a nightlife addict and a mark for all sorts of confidence men and bogus stock salesmen. He lost his money, his practice; then his wife divorced him. When last I heard about him, he had remarried and again was an obscure and struggling doctor in a small midwest town.

Although the doctor's good fortune was a fleeting one, mine was not. My figure improved until I wore a full size smaller than when I was married.

Father never mentioned my obesity to me, nor do I think it made the slightest difference to him. The only time I ever asked him about it he seemed a little surprised.

"I think you know that it is you that I love and not the size of your clothes, my dear," he said. I never mentioned it again.

Nevertheless, he was proud of me when I became slimmer. After we came north that year, a friend of ours arranged a banquet in our honor. So far as I knew, none of the guests had seen me as yet, so Father and I decided to have some fun with them.

He entered the dining room first. After he was seated he made his excuses for my tardiness. While he was talking, I came into the room, ignoring him. I walked slowly to the head of the table. Sure enough, no one recognized me.

My place, next to my host, was vacant and I stood nearby, looking at it expectantly. Without saying a word, however, for I knew my voice would expose me. After a few minutes the silence became strained. It was obvious that everyone wondered why I was there but no one dared ask me about it. Finally the lady in charge of the private dining rooms appeared and politely inquired if I was sure I was in the right room. Still no answer from me. I never looked at her while she diplomatically tried to get me away.

Finally the host said, "Oh, you might as well seat her next to me. She is much better looking than Mrs. Mather-Smith anyway." At that I laughed and gave myself away.

Figure 6.3. Grace after diet. Reproduced courtesy of the Winter Garden
Heritage Foundation.

The guests were speechless and my host appeared chagrined. I often
have wondered: Do you suppose he recognized me at sight and made that
remark to end the embarrassing moment? I don't know, really.

That evening was a grand success for me. The men took up a collection
to persuade the orchestra to play for an additional two hours, while each of
them danced with me. In the past, many of them had dodged me, I know,
on account of my size. Father, with that twinkle which was always there
when I was enjoying myself hugely, had the happiest evening of all.

Incidentally, it was that group of women who started the doctor on his
climb to phantom fortune.

My new figure also caused me some humiliation. Father and I were
train-bound into the city one morning, when my friends commenced to
smile and ask if I had seen this morning's paper. I had not, but as soon as
we left the train, we bought one.

The black headlines on the society page read, "MRS. MATHER-
SMITH, FAMOUS BEAUTY, REDUCES BY WEARING RED FLAN-
NELS AND DOING HER OWN WASH."

I was sure I never could look anyone in the face again, so Father took me for a trip to Boston. When we returned they were talking about someone else and the incident was forgotten. Today, all my inhibitions have vanished. I now would enjoy laughing with them under the same circumstances. Yes, and I probably would carry the red flannels around to show them.

Chapter Seven

Back in Oakland

ORANGE COUNTY FAIR

The next winter was the event of the first Orange County Fair in Orlando.[1] The plan was to have every town in Orange as well as the surrounding counties participate. Sanford, Deland and Apopka furnished displays, as did a number of towns south of us. In spite of the local apathy, Oakland also was represented. Father and I built the booth, trimmed and operated it, while Mother registered the guests.

Mr. Sadler[2] furnished the oranges which we gave to all who stopped. Mr. L.W. Tilden, senior,[3] contributed bearing banana trees, delivered all the way from his home to Orlando by mule-drawn wagons.

Father arranged for the ice plant in Winter Garden to furnish us with huge cakes each day, into which were frozen large bass from Lake Apopka. Other cakes contained encased roses or orange blossoms.

We displayed cabbages large enough to supply a family for days, beets like soft-balls and carrots almost long enough for walking sticks, in addition to choice celery, beans and other vegetables. At the front of the booth we dispensed our oranges to all who registered. Our display was the hit of the show the first day. Then Sanford, who were exhibiting directly across the aisle, made their bid for the crowds. They provided a huge mound of

---

1. The first Orange County Fair was held in February 1911, when the population of Orlando was 4,000.

2. No doubt James Hardy Sadler, the pillar of the Oakland community mentioned in the Editor's Preface.

3. Luther Willis Tilden, son of Luther Fuller Tilden, early pioneer and founder of Tildenville, also mentioned in the Editor's Preface.

EDGEGROVE FARMS

Oakland•Orange County•Florida

Figure 7.1.   Label for Edgegrove Farms produce featuring Grace in a dress decorated with citrus fruit. Reproduced courtesy of the Winter Garden Heritage Foundation.

salt and gave celery to the passers-by. They stole our thunder in a hurry. We did almost no business that day.

That night in our rooms at the San Juan Hotel,[4] we made plans to again lure the crowds to our side. Next afternoon I cut each orange in two so it had to be eaten on the spot. The scheme worked to perfection. Visitors would eat the salty celery and then dash over to us for an orange to quench their thirsts. And they stayed for a second one and a visit in between.

---

4. In downtown Orlando.

At that time, comparatively few people were acquainted with the various varieties of citrus fruit. Neophite though I was, I lectured blithely on the advantages of mixed plantings. When a listener asked about the origin of the pineapple orange which I had been praising to the skies, I blandly explained that it was the result of crossing an orange tree with a pineapple plant. No one corrected me and I was so pleased with this inspirational piece of information that I included it in my lectures for the balance of the afternoon. Then Father overheard it while he waited to take me to dinner. From then on I submitted my lecture subject matter before springing it on the public.

Each night at ten minutes to ten, the lights would flicker off and on as a signal that but ten minutes remained until lights out. Then came a hurried passing of the hat among the concessions to bribe the electricians so that we might accommodate the crowds. And, incidentally, ten o'clock was curfew as far as the electric lights were concerned in Oakland also. We got our power from the plant in Winter Garden and whenever the warning flicker came and we were entertaining, Father had to call the station and make financial arrangements with those on duty there.

I had sent to Chicago for a special dress for the fair. Plum colored it was, and tight fitting. With it, I wore a wide brimmed flamingo hat. I was the best dressed woman for miles around until the evening when I left the booth for dinner and met a disreputable looking man from one of the shows along the carnival midway.

His loud checked suit went well with his canary yellow tie and matching hat band on his stiff brimmed straw hat. The only things that I remember about his face were his potato-like red nose and his mouth full of gold teeth which were juggling an ivory tooth pick.

He fell into step alongside me and said, "Some class, babe. How come I haven't seen you around before? Which outfit are you with?"

I never wore that dress again.

PARENT TEACHERS ASSOCIATION

Each night before we closed we sold the vegetables and fish. The money was turned over either to the hospital in town or to the school fund for our school in Tildenville.

I do not exaggerate when I say that no institution was in need of as many things as our school. Supervised by a board which was handicapped by an almost total lack of funds, and probably lacking fire because its members could not fully appreciate the need for more advantages than they had enjoyed as youngsters, proper aid for the children and teachers suffered.

The school boards of today concern themselves almost exclusively to those matters that have to do with the students. They are content to let the laws of society govern the actions of the teachers. But many years ago, I remember one of our instructors being discharged for, of all things, having a calendar displaying a nude woman in his home. I do not recall that there were any complaints regarding his ability as a teacher.

And at that time, it was a failing, not peculiar to Florida, for small communities to leave all matters pertinent to education and child welfare to the discretion of the governing board. There was no organized interest on the part of the parents to participate toward a better understanding with the school authorities. So that became a project of mine. I organized the School Improvement Association and invited all of the parents to enroll. That group became the P.T.A.

Response was slow until after I drilled a deep well for the children to use in place of the contaminated surface-water well the school provided. After that the parents seemed to get the idea and our membership increased rapidly.

Lack of funds to initiate a definite project threatened to dissolve our organization before the end of its first year. A donation would have been easy but would not provide the necessary incentive. It occurred to me to ask Yowell and Drew's for a donation of remnants which we could sell. They responded with a huge boxfull. These, together with a few things I furnished, were the stock for our Great Remnant and Rummage Sale. We sold every piece and finished with twenty dollars to which Father added another five. Twenty-five dollars was a significant sum in those days. After that we had a comparatively easy time of it. It is heart-warming to recall how proud the youngsters were when their mothers became members and even officers in our association.

Chapter Eight

Edgegrove Farms

Our home in Florida grew with each of you. In addition, it grew on whim and inspiration. From its original five rooms to eight, then ten, twelve and so on to its present twenty-two. And always we extended the house to the west. That sounds like a back-handed gesture to Mecca but in reality it was because of the palm.

Before we were married Father brought me a tiny palm in an ornamental pot. He had no idea that it would thrive in the variable climate of a northern home and he told me so. I was determined that it should. I coaxed it along with almost greenhouse exactness. How carefully I watered it and carried it from room to room to take advantage of as much sunlight as possible, always protecting it from drafts and cold.

It lived and we brought it to Florida. So that we might always see it, we planted the palm just outside the dining room window on the east side of the house. The spot evidently was an ideal one for it took root and grew and grew. It is there today, over forty feet high, with a trunk almost three feet in diameter. The original pot rests beside it. That tree, and our reluctance to move it, is the reason we have always built to the west.

Each new room immediately became part of the whole and behaved just as if it had always been there. I never had the feeling that I was living in a recently remodeled house. As our home grew in size, the number of our guests became greater. As a result we had happier and more joyous seasons each year.

As you know, my dears, I began collecting antique furniture, rugs, paintings and ornaments almost before you were born, but after we built the Columbia dining room I sought additional pieces in earnest.

Figure 8.1.   The 22-room house at Edgegrove Farms. Reproduced courtesy of the Winter Garden Heritage Foundation.

The Columbia room is, or rather was, a replica of the original dining room in our home in Tennessee. To reproduce the exact ceiling height— so necessary to accommodate the two immense crystal chandeliers—we built the floor level some five feet lower than the rest of the house.

The furniture used by David and Ann is there. The huge table where twenty-four guests were easily accommodated at for dinner; the chairs where two generations had eaten in polite silence each evening rest beneath the chandeliers which once were candle-lighted. Talking or levity then were punished by immediate dismissal from the table to eat in the kitchen, and even there, in silence. The ample china cabinet where the Lowestoft china was placed, piece by piece, after every dinner with never a chip or crack, still holds this precious dinnerware.

For two generations, the lady of the house, first Grandma and then Mother, remained seated at the end of each dinner while the servants brought basins of water to the table. Each piece was washed, rinsed, dried and placed in the cabinet before any other tasks could be considered.

The small table in the corner of the room was built for and used by the family slaves. Actually the slaves were made free men at the end of the war, but many of the older ones were unable to comprehend the change and considered themselves slaves until they died.

I have added, from time to time, other pieces to this room, each of which seemed to belong in such fine old company.

The tremendous mirror opposite the entrance is an heirloom from the Mather-Smith home. It is one of the pieces which, along with the silver, was carried to the bank of the lake during that night of terror that was the Chicago fire.[1] Covered with blankets kept soaked from the lake water all night and all next day, they were preserved. When we shipped the mirror south, it became lost along the route somewhere. The express company searched for two years before it was finally located in a warehouse of forgotten and unclaimed items.

The Madonna of the Chair, by Raphael, is an exact copy of that famous work of art. Its two-feet wide frame is carved from one solid piece of oak, as is the original, and the gold leaf overlay is also a faithful replica.

The Audubon print is an original. Audubon made it while in Florida.[2]

The two Girandole mirrors, both very old, Father brought me from France. Or more correctly, he presented them to me there. For although we did not get to Europe for a honeymoon, we visited there many times later.

During one trip, our first one abroad, I was entranced by one wonderful evening under the stars in a gondola in Venice. To commemorate the occasion, Father bought the two candle lamps from the gondolier. They are now mounted on the wall on either side of the entrance to the Columbia room.

We found some of our antiques during our trips abroad but we always had better luck finding them in this country. Once in Italy, I bought a marvelous Italian black marble-topped table. We searched high and low for a Capo di Monte jewel case to adorn it but none could be found outside the museums. When we returned to Chicago, Father bought a perfect one from an impoverished Italian opera singer who needed the money to pay her board bill. The Art Institute wanted it badly but they hesitated too long over the price. Some time later we located an exact duplicate among the effects of an American lady who had lived long in Paris. She had shipped her things to Nashville preparatory to moving back home. She died before her treasures could be uncrated. They now rest together on my black table. As a pair, they are priceless.

For our collection of bronzes, we found some fine Russian, Italian, Japanese and Chinese pieces in Italy, France and England, but the trea-

---

1. The Great Chicago Fire burned from Sunday, October 8, to early Tuesday, October 10, 1871. Of the city's 300,000 inhabitants, 100,000 were left homeless.
2. 1831–32.

sure of them all, my famous troika horses, we located in New York. The story is that the sculptor labored for three years to attain the perfection he demanded for this piece. Then twenty castings were made before this one received his critical approval.

My crystal goblets also have a storied history although they are not antiques.

I was charmed by a display of goblets at the shop of an artisan in glass in Milan and entered, intending to buy twelve of a particular pattern. But the artiste would not consider selling me the ones I had chosen. He insisted that they did not match my personality. For that reason, I might not have them. It required some imagination on my part to appreciate the importance of glassware to harmonize with one's personality. But he was extremely serious and begged me to return the following day when he would have sketches of a glass he was sure I would enjoy owning.

The sketch was of a tall, graceful goblet with tiny pink roses entwined above and below a pale green dolphin on the stem. He had prepared a rosebud for my approval. The workmanship was exquisite so I ordered a dozen glasses.

When he delivered them he emphasized that the design was expressly mine. That if ever a replacement was necessary, not only my signature but the fragments of the piece as well, must be sent to him.

It was inevitable that one glass should be broken soon after we returned. A friend was planning to leave for Italy so I asked him to secure a replacement for me. However, I had neglected to follow instructions so the Italian refused to duplicate the piece. Later, after I had sent the pieces and the written request, I received my glass.

I paid twenty-five dollars each for the original lot but the artist charged fifty dollars for the last one. Still later, when we were in Italy, I ordered two more replacements. For these he charged seventy-five dollars. The man has since died and I understand the secret of his particular art died with him.

Chapter Nine

Family Trip to Europe

Do you remember the trip we all made to Europe in 1923? Do you recall the hectic days preceding it?

We came to New York days ahead of Father who was delayed with business matters. We had Nanny with us and we had a suite of four rooms at the Pennsylvania Hotel.

Early on Sunday morning the manager called me and said that the occupant of room 16 was causing a disturbance. Would I please see that it was stopped at once. Room 16 was Mather's room. It was located on a corner facing a court.

I hurried in and found Mather[1] sound asleep—or so he appeared. Shortly the manager called again, insisting that the disturbance be stopped IMMEDIATELY.

Again Mather was sleeping peacefully. The third time the manager appeared in person. He was a friend of ours so he was very apologetic, but he was positive that the trouble was coming from number 16.

We tiptoed in and caught Mather in the act of soaking newspapers in his bathtub, preparatory to wadding them into balls and throwing them across the court into the bedrooms of sleeping occupants. He had gone into the hall and gathered all of the thick Sunday papers at the doors of the adjacent rooms, for ammunition.

His story—and I believe him—was that he was making paper. He knew that paper started with paper pulp so he was making the pulp in the tub. When he was in danger of being caught, he first tried to run the mass down the drain. It would not pass into the pipe, of course, so he got fright-

---

1. Age 11.

Figure 9.1. Family passport photo taken in 1923

ened and started to toss it out the window. The open bedroom windows across the court were too great a temptation to pass up.

On Monday I took Grace Mary to have her hair done and arranged to meet Nanny with the rest of the family at a certain entrance to the hotel at a specified time. I never have had a very perfect sense of direction so I managed to arrive at the wrong entrance. No family in sight.

Then I saw a crowd gathered before another entrance and went over.

There was Mather pretending he was a blind Negro, clog dancing. Nanny was laughing uproariously while she and Ann took up a collection from the crowd. That afternoon, a friend took Mather horseback riding in Central Park but he was back home in less than an hour. The ride was too tame—he couldn't find anyone to race against.

The ride on the upper deck of a Fifth Avenue bus was also—for Mather—a waste of time and terribly boring until he reached the zoo.

There he went into a cage in the snake house as soon as the attendant wandered far enough away. When we found him he was standing in the center of the snake cage with a king snake draped around his neck and one in either hand. He was lecturing the awe-struck crowd on the art of snake-handling. He knew they were non-poisonous and otherwise harmless but his audience did not; to them a snake, any snake, was sudden death.

By the time Father arrived on sailing day, you all were too excited about the voyage to be anything but model children.

Was the name of our ship, the Lapland?[2] I know we landed at Antwerp from where we first made a brief tour of Holland. Although it could not impress you, Father was intensely interested in the tremendous system of dikes which the ingenious Dutch had erected over so many years to control the attacks of the sea on their tiny nation. The same dikes which they ruthlessly opened again to the sea in the vain effort to stem the advance of the invaders during World War II.

You were much more impressed with the baggy trousers and the wooden shoes of the inhabitants and in the stiffly starched upper-garments and ornate headgear of their women. You were entranced by their custom of scrubbing, not only their front steps in the morning, but the sidewalks and streets as well.

They, in turn, were only mildly interested in our clothes and habits. But they were more than curious over my inevitable parasol. This one had a carved and colored parrot's head handle. More than once that parasol, or rather, the parrot's head, caused a near riot.

We bought Ann's hope chest before we left Holland. And on that trip I obtained many of my Staffordshire figures in England, including my Garibaldi, Napoleon and the rare Emperor Fritz William Hohenzollern. Some of my rarest Toby Jugs we found, oddly enough, in France.

---

2. The SS Lapland was launched in 1908 and was owned by the Red Star Line. She sailed between New York City and Antwerp.

During the crossing to Holland we became friends with a titled English-
man who had been visiting in America. He was a charming gentleman.
We dined at the same table aboard ship and we became very friendly.

We learned that his wife had died a few years before. He was distressed
over his inadequacy to be both a father and a mother to his two children,
a boy and a girl.

He was an immensely wealthy man and repeatedly declared that he
could provide everything in this world for them except the love and attention of a mother.

After we reached Holland we discovered that his itinerary and ours
were identical. Although I was a bit embarrassed because he directed so
much of his attention to me, Father was happy when he proposed that we
visit the continent as a party.

When we crossed from France to England he was so helpful in finding
suitable quarters for us in London. We were to visit his estate for dinner
before we sailed for home.

We were awed by the magnificence of his home. It was located in the
midst of acres of formal gardens; a modernized castle. I became weary
wandering through parlors, sitting rooms, ballroom, gun rooms, library,
morning rooms and game rooms. We ate in a dining room which surely
could have accommodated a hundred guests.

He was a perfect host and his children were as charming as their father.

As we prepared to leave he said, with the candor and abruptness so
characteristic of the English, "No doubt you have observed my atten-
tiveness to your wife. I am rated as one of the wealthiest men in the
Empire. With your permission, I should like to arrange a divorce for
you in London. I want her to become the mother for my children. I can
do so much more for her than you can. Your children will live in the
guest house and have every educational and social advantage. Shall we
arrange it?"

I never was more proud of Father than I was at that moment.

He answered, "I cannot tell you how much we have enjoyed your beautiful estate and I thank you for a perfect evening. Regarding my wife—
that deserves some thought on her part. It is entirely her decision to make.
Good evening, sir."

From his expression and tone of voice I knew Father was not disturbed
about my decision. He was pitying the man.

I think Father knew that something like this would happen some day. He never under-rated the possibility of my attracting the serious attentions of someone else, but he never tried to curb my doing as I pleased on any occasion. A favorite expression of his was, "Grace is like a thoroughbred horse. She is always out there in the limelight. Why shouldn't others enjoy watching her and being near her."

That feeling, in many ways, exemplified Father's philosophy for living. He never, never tried to regulate the life of anyone. He wanted every man to enjoy a happy life although he realized that it might not always be possible. It really pained him that each man would not have what he most desired. "The best friend an underdog ever had," was the comment of a friend.

Our return trip on the S. S. Belgenland was uneventful except for one uneasy afternoon.

Everyone dressed for tea each day. The ladies in gowns, hats, gloves and pocketbooks, and the men in striped trousers and afternoon coats. We had just dressed this afternoon and were passing the bulletin board on deck when Father noticed a sign:

SWIMMING EXHIBITION
FLORIDA CRAWL   WATERMELON SPLIT
BY CHARLES FREDERIC MATHER-SMITH II
TEA WILL BE SERVED IMMEDIATELY AFTER THIS EXHIBITION

According to Father's watch, we only had three minutes to reach the pool. Just as we entered the room Mather, who was on the diving board, was announcing—"I will first demonstrate the watermelon split." Then he leaped into the air and spread-eagled into the pool with a splash which would have done credit to a veteran hippopotamus. I hate to remember how many gowns and striped trousers were ruined that day. Needless to say, tea was NOT served immediately after that exhibition!

I sincerely hope that I am not branding Mather as a problem child. He was a perfectly normal boy who was sometimes bored to distraction from continually being in the company of three or more females.

In retrospect, I do not recall that Mather gave me any more cause for anxiety than you did, my darling daughters.

TRIP TO HOLLYWOOD

Was it not you, Ann, or was it Mable Hudson, who suggested your famous trip to Hollywood when you were youngsters?

One day I discovered that Ann, along with eighteen of my best dresses, most of my hats, shoes and various odds and ends, had disappeared.

Thinking about it today, there does not seem to be much reason to suspect kidnapping, in view of the amount of clothing involved. But after a search of the town failed to provide any clues as to your whereabouts, I was sure that some of the Italian laborers working on the railroad right-of-way through Oakland, had stolen you. These poor innocents had just been imported from Italy and knew no English. They could comprehend the implications of a shotgun aimed at them and they were terrified as I ran among them demanding to know which of them had taken you. The foreman pleaded with me not to kill them one by one, as they were innocent. He swore that not one of them had been out of his sight all day long. He offered to knock off work and turn his crew to the task of searching. I would not permit that. I was only half convinced that they were not guilty.

The men from town formed posses and searched the lake shore and woods for hours with no results.

Long after nightfall, one posse came upon some of my dresses, water-soaked, along the shore. Then we were sure you had drowned.

Hours later, a group of searchers found you huddled in the stern of a rowboat, far across the lake. You had started for Hollywood by rowboat and were waiting for daylight to continue the journey across Lake Apopka. You were not at all abashed at the furor you had been causing.

I was so thankful over your safety that I completely forgot to give you what you deserved.[3]

---

3. Grace's daughter Annie reports that this tale has benefited from substantial embellishment. She says that she and her friend Ruth Hudson in fact planned to abscond to Colorado, not to Hollywood. First they were going to Winter Garden by rowboat; then they were going to follow the railroad tracks to Colorado. But they soon lost the oars to the rowboat and had to abandon their adventure and return home. Annie says that Nanny found her in the bathtub, where she was trying to clean up, and gave her what she deserved.

Chapter Ten

Carmen

With some risk of boring you with repeated references to my singing, I want to tell you about my "Carmen."

You all were quite small the year that a group of Orlando music lovers decided to present a condensed version of the famous opera in an attempt to raise money for the hospital there.

I had appeared in concerts in Orlando on numerous occasions and belonged to the group of that city, so it was suggested that I sing the role of Carmen.

A famous Chicago impressario (fortunately wintering in Florida, or we never could have afforded him) was to direct the piece and local singers were to be the cast.

Figure 10.1. Grace posing in costume as the fiery gypsy Carmen in Bizet's opera. Reproduced courtesy of the Winter Garden Heritage Foundation.

I knew most of the arias and under most circumstances could have taken any part. But not a public showing of Carmen! That was the favorite role of my star of stars, Madame Bériza. Whenever I thought of Carmen I thought of her magnificent interpretation, and then I got tingly chills.

I tried to suggest another singer for the lead. She refused point blank and threatened to leave the cast if it was mentioned again. My friends coaxed and I demurred. I tried every excuse I could call to mind. My voice was not adequate. My social and household duties would not permit me to learn the score in time.

I had to accept when two friends, Mr. and Mrs. Lochlin, who were also members of the cast, proposed that I take the score and go aboard their yacht to insure complete privacy. At the end of a week of constant practice with my hosts I was letter perfect.

The operetta was so well received that we were forced to repeat the performance on two additional evenings.

The following spring, almost as soon as we arrived in Chicago, I learned that this same director was casting for a performance of Carmen. The opera was to be presented at Ravinia Park.[1] This time it was not to be a capsule adaptation. The full score was to be sung, and the internationally famous tenor Octave Dua was to be Don Juan.

I was thrilled to be asked to sing the role of Carmen once more.[2] We started rehearsals and Octave was charmed with the manner in which my voice responded to the mood of the part. In fact, his enthusiasm seemed contagious for most of the company said nice things about my voice, an unusual reaction among opera singers, you can be sure.

Signor Dua also was an admirer of Madame Bériza's wonderful voice. He had performed opposite her on many occasions and professed to be a close friend.

I never have known whether he contacted Madame Bériza or whether it just happened, but after the final rehearsal—the one with full orchestra— my shining star came backstage and told me she had heard the entire score

---

1. The Ravinia Festival takes place in Ravinia Park in Highland Park, Illinois. It opened in 1904 and is the oldest outdoor music festival in the United States, with a series of performances held every summer from June to September.

2. According to the records of the Ravinia Festival, both Madame Bériza and Octave Dua performed in the production of Carmen during the summer of 1916, but there is no mention of Grace's performance that year. Madame Bériza appeared in Carmen at the Ravinia Festival in 1917, as well, but Octave Dua did not. Since Grace says that she performed with Octave Dua and that Madame Bériza not only attended her final rehearsal but lent Grace her costumes for the role, it seems likely that Grace substituted for Madame Bériza in 1916.

from the front of the house. She was enchanted with my interpretation and insisted that I wear her original costumes for the part.

I was lifted to heaven by her praise and I am sure that I sang as never before, the night of the performance. At the curtain of the second act, Don Juan, to whom I had been directing my song, rose from his seat and applauded with the audience.

After the performance, the director of the Chicago Symphony Orchestra, who played the score, also came backstage and paid me the compliment of declaring that he never had heard a better rendition of the part. His praise was best, next to Madame Bériza's, for he had directed for most of the great stars. Thank heaven that Madame Bériza had not remembered me as the tongue-tied girl of a few years before. When I called to thank her for loaning me her beautiful costumes, she insisted that I go back to New York with her for auditions at the Metropolitan. She was even more insistent that I accompany her to Paris where she owned two opera houses. She was full of enthusiastic plans which, she said, would assure me of a future of success.

A few days after the performance, two gentlemen from Steinway Hall in New York called and offered me a most flattering contract for a series of solo concerts, the first of which was to be at Steinway Hall.

Mother insisted that I sign without delay. This was the culmination of everything she had visualized. She had long since forgotten her earlier antipathy for the concert stage and the theatre.

I discussed the contract with Father and he responded as whole-heartedly as always.

"You must do whatever you think will result in the greatest happiness for you. By all means, make the tour if that is what you want to do. Only consider it carefully first. Don't let the gentlemen stampede you into a hasty answer. Take a few days before you see them again."

Instead of the few days he suggested, it took me only a few minutes to make my decision. I lived, not for the concert stage any more, but only for my devoted family. Domesticity and the love of my dear ones were the only things that mattered. A few years and fame would pass me by as she was now passing another to give me my hour on her pinnacle. In the meantime, I should have lost the thing which counted for so much more in my life.

I have been told by many (including Madame Bériza) that I was born for the concert stage and the opera and never for family life. But my life has been so full as I have lived it that I have proven they were wrong. Obviously so, for I have had both. I enjoyed my momentary peak of success and I still have the love of my family.

Mother did not accept my decision with grace. She was bitter in her comments concerning the wisdom of my refusal.

She told me, "After I die, you never will sing again." Not long afterward she died suddenly, at a bridge game in Orlando.[3] There were two doctors present but nothing could be done to save her life.

After the shock of her passing and I tried to sing again, her prophecy stirred in my subconcious and locked the fluidity of my singing voice. I never sang again.

Today the psychiatrists would have fixed that condition in a hurry, I suppose.

---

3. In or around 1918.

Chapter Eleven

Trip Back West

And do you remember when I took the three of you and Nanny to Denver?

Ann had an asthmatic tendency that did not respond to local treatment. When our doctor suggested taking her to Colorado, I decided at once on Denver. It met the doctor's requirements regarding altitude and I was anxious to renew old acquaintances. I had been there but once, and then only fleetingly, since marrying Father.

But just as I had forsaken Denver for Chicago, so had my friends married and moved to Boulder, to Pueblo, Greeley and to Colorado Springs.

We had come west by train so the only way to get to all of the places which seemed important at the time was by car. I bought a Hudson Super-Six touring car and in it we proceeded to enjoy the sights and the cities which once had been nothing but horrendous geography conundrums.

Figure 11.1.   Grace, her three children and Nanny in rear two rows of White Motor Company open touring bus at Yellowstone Park in 1926

Figure 11.2. Grace, her children and Nanny on the summit of Pikes Peak (altitude 14,109 feet) on August 2, 1926

PIKE'S PEAK

While we were visiting an old friend in Colorado Springs I was smitten with an urge to see the top of Pike's Peak.[1] Then, the trip was still a stunt as well as a test of motor performance, usually accomplished by an expert driver together with a mechanic whose duty it was to keep the car in running condition during the grind to the top. The halfway house was not yet completed, the guard[rail]s had not been installed, and the road was in poor shape in many places.

We were warned about all of these things, but we went away just the same. I did not learn until we returned, that I was the first person to make it without a mechanic. Certainly it was providential that the motor and the gears behaved so perfectly that day, for I would have had only the slight-

---

1. Pikes Peak (the apostrophe has been eliminated), which is near Colorado Springs, rises to 14,115 feet above sea level. The highway to the summit was built in 1916; the toll was initially $2. Grace made her ascent on August 2, 1926, as evidenced by the family photograph taken at the summit.

est notion what to do, had anything failed. We should have camped where we were until another thrill-seeker happened along.

The warnings about the condition of the road were all too true. In places it was terrible: rutted and rough, very narrow in spots and forever twisting and turning.

Nanny sat at the outside edge of the rear seat. She had the utmost confidence in anything I did, but she was scared half to death just the same. In the rearview mirror, I could see the whites of her eyes, big as silver dollars, as she watched the edge of the road. She sang spirituals all the way up—no doubt to keep from shrieking aloud.

"Oh Lord," I heard her sing, "I know Miss Grace will get us up there sure enough, but couldn't you push us over just a little tiny bit? These back wheels is throwin' gravel down the mountain side, and maybe Miss Grace don't know that."

The radiator sprayed us from its plumes of steam, the gears groaned and growled in anguish and the tires shuddered as they fought for a firmer grip on the road, but we made it to the peak.

I am afraid that the grandeur of the view was somewhat dimmed for me, by the thoughts of the return trip. Coming down was to be as hazardous as the climb. Four-wheel brakes were still just a dream, so guiding the car around these curves without skidding the rear wheels off the road and at the same time contrive to do it without burning the smoking brakes to cinders was a trick which had to be learned in a hurry.

We were totally unprepared for the sensation we created upon our return. The Colorado Springs Gazette wanted so much to do a feature story on the trip, with emphasis on the ease with which it might be undertaken by a carload of women and children. That, no doubt, was in the interests of the tourist business.

The Hudson people tried hard to have me agree to photographs and a statement for their advertising. But you know me. We had not done it as a stunt, or for the publicity in prospect; we merely wanted to see Pike's Peak from the top. The newspapers did carry the story, but not in any embarrassing way.

We were urged to stay over in Colorado Springs for the party to be given for all those who had driven to the peak and back but we could not arrange it.

CHEYENNE

A month earlier[2] I had engaged hotel accommodations for all of us at the Plains Hotel in Cheyenne, Wyoming.[3] The event was the Frontier Days Celebration and Homecoming Week.[4] The advance publicity promised us parades, fireworks and a rodeo.

Immediately after breakfast on Monday morning we set out from Denver in the car. Although the distance to Cheyenne was only about a hundred miles it was long after noon when we got there. Traffic was heavy and the roads so dusty that we could hardly see.

I never had seen the streets in New Orleans as packed with merrymakers at Mardi Gras time than the main street of this small town. For this week an automobile was a contraption of recent vintage (as it truly was) and as such it must give way to horses, carriages, wagons and pedestrians. I know we could have pushed the car up the street faster than we drove that day.

At last we reached the hotel and parked the car as near the front entrance as possible. As we alighted, Mather screamed with delight at a cowboy in a cerise shirt who was passing at a gallop. The man saw Mather and he galloped over, lifted him with one hand and placed him in the saddle in front of him. Then he shouted and they tore down the streets fast as the crowds would permit.

I was frantic. I tore through that crowd like a banshee. I chased them to the end of the street where they stopped in front of a large corral. There the man dismounted leaving Mather in the saddle alone.

Before I could regain enough breath to utter a word, he bowed, sweeping his Stetson in an arc like a cavalier and said, "Don't be afraid, ma'am, I wouldn't let the little feller get hurt. Not for all the world. You brought him here to have a good time, didn't you?" I stammered that that was the general idea. "Well, he's goin' to have that time and there's no better time to start than right this minute."

---

2. I suspect Grace is combining two different trips to Colorado here, since Mather was 15 when Grace drove the family up Pikes Peak and he is described as a "little feller" when he was in Cheyenne.
   3. The Plains Hotel opened in 1911 and is still operating.
   4. Cheyenne Frontier Days is an outdoor rodeo and western celebration that has been held annually since 1897.

I could not be angry with the man, even when he grinned like an imp and said, "Now I'm goin' to show the little feller some wild horses. Come along. You'll enjoy it."

As we walked toward the corral with Mather still in the saddle he asked where we were staying. I told him that we had reservations at the Plains Hotel and that we would have been in our rooms now if he had not upset our immediate plans.

While Mather watched the wild horses, our new friend pointed to a house far out on the prairie and asked if I could see it. I could—just—although it was the only house in sight.

"That house is mine. After you find out that you cannot stay at the Plains, I would be honored if you and your family will move into that little place for as long a visit as you like. By the time you get there, I will have everything that you need ready for you."

I was sure that there would be no trouble at the hotel and thanked him for his offer.

On the way back to the hotel he said, "You are a good mother and a fine woman. I like the way you fight for your youngsters. I hope I am wrong about your rooms at the hotel, but don't forget about my house if you need it."

As we reached the rest of the family I was forcibly reminded that it was far past lunch time, so I told them that we would eat at a restaurant across the street before we went to our rooms.

Again my friend grinned. "Those three places over there are the only eatin' places in town. How do you figure you are goin' to get your brood into any one of them?" There were long queues in front of each restaurant.

"Great heavens," I cried, "I must have some milk and food for my children. Nanny and I can wait until later."

"I don't think you will find a bottle of milk in the whole town," said the man. He volunteered to try and find something and disappeared. Presently he returned with two beer bottles of milk and two or three hard rolls. "All I could locate," he said. He had found them in a saloon.

When I approached the desk at the hotel and asked for our rooms, the clerk just shook his head sadly. He did not even answer me. I became angry and showed him the letter acknowledging our reservations.

"Lady," he said, "we had about fifty reservations for today and right now we have about fifty very angry people as a result. Hundreds of folks just roamed the halls before daylight this morning and moved into any vacant rooms they found. If you can tell me any way to get them out without getting shot full of holes or getting my face pushed in, you can have the best rooms in the house with my compliments."

Then he braced himself for the angry blast of the man behind me.

Of course, there was nothing we could do about it. Nanny agreed that it was either a case of sleeping in the car—definitely impossible—or taking the house on the prairie.

We went to the hardware store and bought two of the largest butcher knives in stock. Why does a woman always choose a knife as a weapon of defense?

There was no one at home when we arrived. Also, there was little chance that anyone might be lurking nearby, for there were no places of concealment. No trees, no bushes, no barns and hardly any grass. Just a few sagebrush here and there. We were indeed alone on the lone prairie.

The place was small but as neat as one could wish. The beds were ready and there was a note on the table which told us that we could find plenty of food in the cellar below. The cellar was reached through a trap-door in the floor near the stove. We were desperately hungry so Nanny and I cautiously descended the ladder with our butcher knives held at alert. But there was nothing in sight but food: meat, hams, bacon slabs, potatoes, vegetables and a can of very fresh milk.

We prepared our dinner, using the supplies as frugally as possible until we had some understanding regarding it. We left a place at the table for our friend and we waited as long as possible but he did not appear. Nor did we see him during the evening although we waited anxiously, with our knives handy but not visible.

Finally, we locked the door, braced it with a chair under the latch and undressed for bed in darkness. During the night we were chilled speechless by the howls of the coyotes that prowled around but no danger threatened us.

In the morning, we again prepared a place at the table, but again he did not appear. During the morning a cowboy rode up with fresh milk and the word that Mr. Warburton had sent this gentle horse—which he was leading—for the children to ride. Mr. Warburton also warned us that the opening performance of the rodeo started at two that afternoon.

The children certainly did have a grand time with that horse but when we had to get ready for the performance, not one of us had the foggiest notion how to remove his saddle and bridle. So we tied the poor beast to the corner of the house and hoped that someone who knew about such things would tend to it. Our host anticipated our incompetence, for when we returned the horse was gone.

I left the children with Nanny to enjoy the wonders of the fair while I went on to buy our tickets for the rodeo. Mr. Warburton must have described me quite accurately to the ticket man for when I asked for five seats he asked, "Are you the lady with the three kids and a nigger?" I told him I was. "Your tickets have been arranged for. Here you are—Box A."

We found our seats in the most central spot in the grandstand and so close to the arena that Mather was in ecstacy.

Until the announcer shouted that the next event would be "Trick and fancy riding by the World's Champion—Gil Warburton," I had no idea that our host would be one of the performers. Certainly not such a famous one. When he took part in the Roman Race, he waved his hat each time he passed our box.

We waited at the entrance after the performance until everyone had left, hoping our friend would come by so we could thank him for the wonderful afternoon, but he did not appear. Nor did we see him, except in the arena, on subsequent afternoons, although our tickets were presented to us each day with his compliments.

On Saturday, the man at the box office said, "Gil wants me to say that you should not attempt to drive back to Denver after the show. The roads will be jammed, and too dangerous for a lady to travel." On Sunday we again had news that the roads were still crowded and Gil sent word by our milkman that we should remain until Monday.

I took the family to see a large dairy on Sunday. The family who ran the farm had a number of children and they suggested that I drive the car home and let the youngsters return together on horseback.

The sunset that evening was magnificent. I can remember no time in my life when I felt more relaxed and at peace than at that moment, sitting before the house enjoying the glorious solitude. All sounds from the fair and carnival had disappeared; my children were in good company; for the moment, I had not a care in the world.

That was the moment Gil Warburton chose to make his first visit. He rode up so quietly that he was almost beside me before I saw him. When he learned that I was alone he didn't want to stay, but I urged him to sit with me until my family returned, then have dinner with us.

The dinner he declined, just as he refused my thanks for his hospitality.

He answered my questions about his work, his ranch and some of the things I asked about his life. Suddenly he stopped talking. After several minutes of silence he said, "Something tells me I should tell you the real story of my life although I have never told it to a soul before. You are too fine a lady to tell a pack of evasive half-truths." Then he told me a tale as fantastic as a dime novel.

Although many years have passed since that afternoon, I will hold to my agreement never to divulge his real identity nor the name of his home town. In substance, this is his story:

I was standing in front of a livery stable on the main street of the town where I was born, one evening. I was talking to my best friend.

Suddenly a shot was fired from a pistol held just over my right shoulder. My friend fell dead where he stood. In the excitement of the moment, the assassin disappeared, probably into the dark interior of the stable, without my having caught a glimpse of him. There were two men working on their horses in the barn but they testified at the trial that they had not seen the murderer.

I was arrested on the scene and charged with the murder of my friend. My reputation was a good one; I was not a gunman—in fact, I did not own a pistol—nevertheless the evidence was damning.

The angle from which the bullet hit his body indicated that I could have fired the shot. No gun was produced, of course, but that was more than balanced by the fact that only I mentioned the circumstances of the vanished gunman. No motive was proven, but the jury returned a verdict of first degree murder against me and I was sentenced to hang.

My folks had a fair amount of money and considerable influence in the town. They contrived, therefore, to arrange to set me free. Call it a jail break if you like, but actually a number of friends staged a diversion in front of the jail while I walked out an open door in the rear.

But I did not remove myself far enough from my home. I was recognized and brought back so that the sentence could be carried out.

In the meantime, friends of mine and Father's thoroughly worked over the two men who had been in the barn with the result that they admitted seeing the man who had escaped. He was a notorious character, and for that reason they had feared to antagonize him.

The night before I was to be hanged, they discovered where he was hiding. They commandeered a switch engine and one car, rode most of the night to reach his hangout and returned with him hog-tied on the floor. They got the judge out of bed to hear the man's confession and to start the machinery toward my release. ·

I am sure you can understand why I wanted to get away from all people and associations that reminded me of those harrowing days. So now even my name is new. I was christened --------- -----------, but I never will answer to it again. I chose the name Gilbert Warburton from two characters—the hero and the villain—in an old book I came across. I believe it was "Portrait of a Lady."[5] I was fairly sure that by using a garbled fictional name, no one was likely to claim kinship.

I travelled for some time, working at widely separated ranches. I was a good horseman so when ranch work became scarce, I joined a circus as a trick rider. We toured most of this country, then Europe and back to the United States.

I fell in love with and married a lady performer with the show and I thought we would be happy together for the rest of our lives. Until I discovered that her nature was such that she never could be happy with any one man—I was being deceived with regularity. I left her in disgust and we were divorced as rapidly as I could arrange it. I heard later that a jealous wife had shot and killed her.

Since then, my only love has been my ranch and my horses. I now have over two thousand.

The family had come home during the telling of this story, and now their demands for food were so insistent that Mr. Warburton would not stay longer. He asked, however, that we meet him in town in the morning on our way back to Denver.

---

5. Written by Henry James; published in 1881. The villain is Gilbert Osmond, who seduces the novel's protagonist, Isabel Archer, and marries her for her money. The hero is Lord Warburton, who falls in love with Isabel and woos her to no avail.

He was waiting for us at the hotel and after saying goodbye to the children, he asked me to walk to the corner with him. There he ushered me into a jewelry shop with a stock of things as fine as any metropolitan store.

"I should like you to choose the prettiest thing in sight for the prettiest lady I have ever known."

I was bewildered and embarrassed. I refused to consider any gift at all. But he pressed so many arguments that I finally chose an inexpensive pair of "beauty pins," so popular at that time. He was horrified. "I request you to pick any gift, without regard for its cost, and you choose two tiny pins that cannot even impress your children."

I explained that the pins would serve to remind me of his kindnesses as effectively as a tiara. That the acceptance of an important gift would be unfair to my husband and my family. He gravely agreed and reminded me again that he considered me a fine person.

After I reached home and told Father this story, he wrote Mr. Warburton a note which we both signed, thanking him for everything he had done for us, but we never received an answer.

During the early days of the First World War[6] I received a postal card from him saying that he had enlisted and was scheduled for overseas immediately. If he could be of any assistance, he might be reached through his lawyers, whose name he included. We never heard from him again.

---

6. The United States declared war on Germany in April 1917.

Chapter Twelve

Civic Improvements

As long as we lived in Florida Father tried so hard to foster and then develop a spirit of civic pride in the residents of Oakland. Always with failure or indifferent results.

It is a dogma that the natives anywhere resent progress and change, nevertheless it is but fair to say that those in Oakland did have some reasons for their apathy. They had seen the town grow, blossom and then fade.

The railroad had brought prosperity and then taken it away. They could not seem to realize that a permanent growth from another source might be developed with proper effort. For one thing, the tourist traffic was increasing tremendously. Lake Apopka was becoming famous for its fishing and the woods around us abounded with game. But for them, the glory was gone, never to return, so why try.

PARKS

One attempt of ours was the town park. The land across the street from the post office was a sorry-looking low place which was, by common consent, the town dump. Unsightly with its rusting tin cans and at times a little gamey in odor, it truly was an eyesore which confronted every visitor. In spite of Father's comments, some of which were a bit pointed, the town did very little about the condition.

In desperation, he took the spot over as a personal project. Father spent thousands of dollars and eventually developed a really beautiful park. The only contributions asked of the town folks was that they each plant a tree,

Figure 12.1.   Grace Park Depot, Oakland, FL. Reproduced courtesy of the Winter Garden Heritage Foundation.

plant or flower that they particularly liked so that everyone would have an interest there. Some few of them responded, but most didn't bother.

With appropriate ceremony it was christened Grace Park.[1] That was the end as far as many of them were concerned. After all, now it was less convenient to dispose of tin cans and other discarded items. As soon as we stopped maintaining the park, it fell into disuse.

CLUBS

Another project which met with a combination of indifference and indignation was our golf course. Father built the first privately owned club—with the second longest course in the United States—in Oakland.[2] Full eighteen holes, with a more than adequate clubhouse as well as cottages to house our guests. Each cottage was completely furnished, even to the food, drinks and servants. No guest ever was permitted to pay one cent during his stay with us.

---

1. In 1913.
2. The West Orange Country Club opened in 1915.

Figure 12.2.   West Orange Country Club

The guesthouses and our home, which by that time was as large as it now is, were filled pretty much to capacity for most of the winter season. Quite naturally, this did not hurt the local merchants a bit.

The clubhouse with its lockers and showers and the fine course might have been capitalized to the express advantage of a town so badly in need of money for civic improvement. Furthermore, Father was most anxious to cooperate. But again, no concerted interest was developed. In fact, after an indignation meeting[3] Father was restrained from completing five drainage wells on our property. These wells were intended to protect the course from erosion.

During World War I, I tried once more to stimulate an interest in the golf club. There was a need for recreational facilities for the suddenly in-creased population.[4] I hired a golf professional, a manager[5] and a hostess and for a time we ran a full-fledged club. But the drainage between Black Lake, John's Lake and Lake Apopka was inadequate and we, as individu-

---

3. An "indignation meeting" is a meeting held for the purpose of expressing and discussing griev-ances.

4. Due to the construction of military training camps.

5. Every winter the golf pro, Joe MacMorran, came down from the Indian Hill Country Club in Winnetka, Illinois, and the manager, Mrs. Mackin, came down from the Exmoor Club in Highland Park, Illinois.

als, could do nothing about it. The grounds became flooded during the rainy season and we had to abandon the entire project permanently.[6]

By this time, the pattern of official policy was so evident that we never tried to inflict anything more on Oakland.

CHURCHES

On reflection, that is not a completely correct statement because we did improve the complexion of the town later, but in the Negro section. That was my project.

It gave me pleasure, as it does today for that matter, to regard the Negroes as human beings and to see that they received some of the advantages not then available to them.

I felt that I had truly accomplished something when I was one of those who made it possible for the Negroes to have a school for their children.

Next came the churches—two of them.[7] At first we planned to provide a single place of worship to be used in place of the Sunday gatherings in the fields or in the schoolhouse. Then we learned that there were almost equal numbers of Methodists and Baptists. The result was that we provided two churches instead of one.

In spite of my wishes to the contrary, each church displays a large, colored and framed enlargement of "Miss Grace" on its walls. The Negroes never were demanding. When one of the churches needed a new roof, it was left for me to discover that fact. They got their roof and more, although I did not personally provide the money.

Each winter when our house was full of guests, I took them in groups for at least one service at each church. The sincere services were wholesome and the method of conducting them, a novelty. Besides, the churches needed their contributions.

---

6. The club closed in 1924 after three years of heavy rain caused the adjacent John's Lake to rise and flood the property, destroying the golf course. In 1941, Charles Mann "Pete" Tucker acquired the country club property and named it Tucker & Son Ranch, and used it to raise cattle and grow citrus. In 2011, the City of Winter Garden (for the property was now part of Winter Garden) purchased the 209 acre site in order to create a park.

7. The St. Paul Missionary Baptist Church and the Mt. Zion African Methodist Episcopal Church. Grace herself was a member of the Oakland Presbyterian Church.

Figure 12.3. Photographic portrait taken in Hawaii of "Miss Grace" with a pikake lei, which hung in two Oakland churches she helped build

When the question of the new roof was most urgent, I took all of my guests on a particular Sunday. Bertha Baur[8] preached the sermon and you can bet that her subject touched heavily on charity.

Blanche Meigs[9] took up the collection and her contribution set the pattern for the others. We got enough money for the new roof and a regulation pulpit as well. The next day Bertha Baur went into town and relieved the parish of its burden of debt against the church property.

When I heard that the first church wedding was to be performed, I donated the red rug from my living room to help provide the proper atmosphere. Although the rug still is doing duty, there has never been another church wedding.

I always have believed that a man becomes a better citizen if he has some roots in a community. We made it possible for the Negroes to buy

---

8. A friend from Chicago. Her obituary in the New York Times described Mrs. Bertha Duppler Baur (born 1870; died 1967) as a "millionaire, suffragette, lawyer and G.O.P. leader in Illinois."

9. Another Chicago friend, who was married to Merrill C. Meigs (1883-1968), publisher of the Chicago Herald & Examiner and champion of Meigs Field, an airfield only 10 minutes from Chicago's Loop, which opened in 1948. He was also a golfer.

land and build homes in their section of Oakland.[10] The result is that we enjoy one of the most orderly and law-abiding sections to be found.

CASKETS

Certainly some of the Negroes are not homeowners, nor otherwise self-provident; just as there are also indigent whites. Many of each race depart this life with no more assets than when they were born. For this emergency I had an arrangement with an undertaker—there were no morticians then—whereby I enjoyed a rock-bottom price for quantity purchases of a serviceable and presentable casket. I paid twenty-five dollars each for them and altogether I bought hundreds.

Intended only to offer comfort to those who otherwise would have had to depend on a county burial, I soon discovered that I was donating caskets to some who were far from destitute. And also, that the field of my activities was increasing by leaps and bounds. Before long I got requests from as far away as Leesburg.[11] How the word spread so quickly I do not know but I did a land-office business in caskets for a time.

One white family who really needed help lived in Ocoee.[12] When I called my undertaker, he told me that he had just returned from a series of instructions for something very new in our part of the country—embalming. I talked him into a practical demonstration of his art on the old lady who had just died.

Her family were entranced with her appearance. They sent word to friends and relatives for miles around to come and see granny. Her sons told me that she looked so pretty that they hated to bury her. As it was, they kept her around much longer than the health authorities of today would permit.

Embalming was not universally adopted immediately. A natural resistance had to be overcome. And there was the question of superstition to be reckoned with.

---

10. Known as "the Quarters."
11. Thirty miles northwest of Oakland.
12. Six miles east of Oakland, on the far side of Winter Garden.

COMETS

Someone has said that superstition is not the heritage of an age or a race. Rather, it is the acceptance of an explanation, within the reasoning powers of those involved, for a happening otherwise beyond their comprehension. The fact that the explanation usually concerns The Hereafter in some way is easily understood.

One evening Halley's Comet appeared in the sky over our heads.[13] The fiery pinwheel with its long trail of scintillating satellites presented a beautiful sight. There was nothing mysterious about it; certainly nothing supernatural. That is, if you knew what it was.

But some of the natives had never heard of Halley's Comet. What other explanation was there, therefore, but that the heavens were falling and the end of the world was upon us? Here was the vanguard of the fires of destruction.

I was at home enjoying the sight which would not be repeated for another seventy-six years, so I knew nothing of the excitement until a neighbor hurried over and urged me to come up to the post office and prepare for the coming of the end of all things along with the rest of the residents. I went, of course, not to greet doomsday there in the street, but to find out the reason for the prediction.

The sight there was at once ridiculous and sad. Men and women, white and black, were gathered together, each with his treasures, mostly bedding and mattresses, on his back.

"If this is the end, Miss Grace, we are ready," was the theme of their shouts. A great Negro who had been down along the lake shore came running up just as I started to talk to them and not seeing me at once, shouted, "It sure is the Day of Judgement and Miss Grace ain't goin' to wait for the Lord to come. She done crucified her baby, just like Jesus, up on the porch."

What he had seen in the evening light was Grace Mary's little long-sleeved and long-legged sleeping garments drying on a stretcher on the upstairs porch. I managed to get their attention long enough to explain this carefully and then to make them understand the uselessness of heading for heaven with a bundle of bed clothes. Then came a short lecture on the

---

13. May 19, 1910.

wonder that was Halley's Comet which had been predicted by astrono-mers with such accuracy. After I repeated that they were now enjoying a spectacle which would not again be visible for so many years that few of us could hope to witness its next flight through the skies, they left quietly for the homes and their earthly beds.

Chapter Thirteen

Flowers, Fruits and Friends

The minute examination of one's past (as I seem to be doing) is fraught with some danger, my dears.

The discovery that Father and I have lived through periods that have become historical comes as a devastating shock. And the realization that we have contributed to that history—even infinitesimally—is more than slightly frightening. Those years have each slipped by with no more blatant warning than my mirror has given of the approaching twilight of my life.

My kind and gentle friends, Doctor Alfred Hanna and his charming wife, Doctor Kathryn Abbey Hanna,[1] whose many fascinating books about Florida's history are rapidly becoming textbooks for other historians, undoubtedly consider forty odd years as a mere yesterday. But to me they have contained much history.

Long before Texas was producing pink grapefruit, Father was successfully growing them by grafting the native grapefruit tree with the ruby orange. Pollination was a hobby of his and he developed a limequat, with a flavor far superior to the lime, by a combination of pollination and hybriding.

We had the first white poinsettias in the interior and the first pink ones. The brick-red bougainvillea—the one at the inner gates—which is now over forty feet tall, is another first. It is now past forty years old.

We also were the first to plant jacarandas, gardenias, blue and red salvia and the pink bohemias. We had well over a hundred different blooming plants in the garden and fifty-four varieties of fruits and nuts on our land.

---

1. Dr. Alfred J. Hanna was a leading scholar on Florida history and a professor at Rollins College for 40 years. His wife, Dr. Kathryn Abbey Hanna, was another leading Florida historian and chair of the History Department at Florida State University for 15 years.

I have added to them ever since although many of the original ones have lived their lives and had to be removed. I will not try to guess the number of living varieties we have today.

My very rare sausage tree—a holy tree from India—has been hand pollinated and will bear its strange fruit this year. My new leech tree has taken root and is throwing out its first new growth. I continually add to my medicinal garden with its bitter aloes, bella donna, cocaine, deadly nightshade, sapodilla and so many others whose names are spelled and pronounced most easily by a pharmacist. My Brazilian coffee tree is so heavily laden with fruit that we must prop each limb against breaking.

A letter today from Doctor Hamilton Holt[2] reminds me of the number of years I have enjoyed his friendship. The State of Florida owes much to Doctor Holt for the position Rollins College occupied among the country's significant schools. Doctor Holt's incomparable wisdom, humor and his realistic understanding of life's problems are a continual revelation to me.

Here and there, among these pages, I have mentioned by name a few of my friends. I am sad that I cannot remember each one by some mention here, but they number so many that the result would resemble a telephone directory. In my heart I treasure them all as my most priceless possessions.

Reminiscence over the variety and the kindnesses of my friends has brought on a period of meditation. And from it comes the problem of how best to tell you of the balls, the parties and the dinners I have enjoyed. Surely you can understand that I cannot count them, for there were thousands. From Chicago to Florida, San Francisco to Hawaii, and from New York to London and Paris.

Any effort to describe one of a few would be an injustice and destroy the flavor of them all. In my memory they are a *matchless rope of pearls.* Each one perfect by itself but most magnificent in the company of the others. There each small one—each tiny one—is as important and beautiful as the largest.

---

2. President of Rollins College from 1925 until 1949. Grace was an active supporter of Rollins College, which conferred upon her the honor of "Patron of Rollins College" in 1960. In 1949, she and Dr. Holt carried on a sometimes flirtatious correspondence where he addressed her as "Graciola" (perhaps a play on "gladiola," possibly a favorite flower) and she addressed him as "Hamiltonolo." In one letter, Dr. Holt thanks her for "your good letter, redolent with Graciolaish personality." Graciola certainly had plenty of personality.

Chapter Fourteen

Tales and Tall Tales

THE BOOTLEGGER

For no good reason that I recall, I often helped our doctor in confinement cases. I did pity the poor, overworked man who often was forced to bring babies into the world under almost impossible conditions. Needless to say, he was happy to call me when I could be useful, saying that I was as good or better than a trained nurse.

Babies, of course, arrive according to some celestial schedule which does not always synchronize with convenience, clocks nor the sun and moon. So I with my sheets, soap, washcloths and towels, comb and brush and a nightgown or two for the emergency, was on call at all hours. Often we were called to a home that did not possess a single sheet to say nothing of a nightgown.

One time I was called during a costume party at the club. We all were dressed as children and having a gay time when the doctor appeared at the door. I hurried home to get into some presentable clothes and to pick up my kit.

The family lived some distance from town. In fact, it was almost to Minneola.[1] And ever so far back in the woods. The husband had ridden to town on horseback and then started back immediately.

He met us at the side road leading to his home and proceeded on his horse, leading us through an almost impassable jungle over a road which was a mere path.

---

1. About 10 miles west of Oakland, on Lake Minneola.

I can be excused for being a little frightened. I was sure that the doctor was handier with his pills and scalpel than he would be with his fists and the man did look like the personification of all of the brigands in the world.

He carried a litard knot[2] to show us the way and its weird flame accented his fearsome features each time he looked our way. To complete his character, he punctuated all of his remarks with robust oaths. And when no conversation was required he ad-libbed strings of disconnected cuss-words for no reason whatsoever.

It seemed miles that we lurched over logs and roots and spun our wheels madly through bogs. Each one minutely and explosively described by our guide and pin-pointed with his flare.

At last we reached his clearing to see a ramshackle house with three children asleep on the floor and the mother lying in a home-made bed with her new baby which had arrived while we were hurrying through the woods. There was much to do, both for the doctor and me, and it was nearly morning when we climbed back into the car. The husband came out and asked how much the doctor's charge was.

"Fifty dollars," said he. "Cash."

I was horrified. While it was true that the house was well stocked with food of good quality, there was little else to suggest that the family had any money at all. But the doctor sat there complacently while the husband roared an entirely new collection of smoking words. Finally, he quieted, went into the house and returned with the money. He handed it to the doctor just as he was asking me, "Did you remember to bring the Kelly pad,[3] Mrs. Mather-Smith?"

"Hey, wait a minute. Are you that rich Mather-Smith woman, over in town?"

The doctor told him that I was the only Mrs. Mather-Smith in Oakland.

"Well, you're no nurse and besides, I didn't ask for no nurse, but I suppose I got to pay you just the same for what you done. How much?"

"Mrs. Mather-Smith has come along to help me and to do those things that no doctor ever can do proficiently. She does not get paid either by you or me. You should thank her."

---

2. A pine knot burned as a torch light.
3. A medical device used to help detect postpartum hemorrhage.

The husband glared at me for a moment and then went into the house without a word.

On the way home I remonstrated with the doctor over the amount he had charged the poor man.

"Don't you worry about that. There are plenty of my patients who haven't got a dime to pay for a doctor, but this fellow is a well-to-do man for this section. He operates a still back there in the woods some-where—makes first-rate liquor, too—also he is a poacher and does other things where his materials cost him nothing and his profit is high. He doesn't understand the need for conveniences as we know them, and for that, his family must suffer. But make no mistake about it, he could afford them."

Late that fall, one of the maids came to me one evening to say that there was a terrible-looking man at the door who refused to talk with anyone but me.

It was my friend, the husband, as disreputable-appearing as before and as blasphemous. He never gave me a chance to inquire about his wife or family, but blurted out, "Can you keep your mouth shut about something that only me and you must ever know?"

I refused to commit myself and tried to find out just what he had in mind. But he insisted on my promise of secrecy first.

I suspected that he wanted me to perform an abortion from the way he was acting. Unthinkable, even if I did know how, but to get rid of him I agreed to keep quiet, making a mental reservation to get out of it somehow later.

He led me to the rear of his wobbly wagon and said, "Where will I put 'er?"

I looked blankly at him.

"That there barrel is full of the finest corn whisky in Florida." He spat on the drive and then, "I know, because I made 'er myself."

For the next five years, he came each fall. Not with more moonshine but each time with a load of the grandest vegetables imaginable. His lan-guage never improved one bit, nor did his appearance. His wagon became more delapidated each time. After that I never saw him again. Whether the law finally caught up with him or whether he just decided that his account with me was paid, I do not know.

But I do know that some of my friends were deeply shocked when I told them about my visitor (leaving out the part about the barrel), because they all know him and his unsavory reputation.

I have discovered that a shocking tale, sometimes true as is this one, but more often a fiction, will often save an otherwise embarrassing situation.

"WILD PLUM"

Shortly after the war, while some of the restrictions were still in force, I gave a luncheon for Grace Mary at the hotel in Orlando. We had it there because of the difficulty with gasoline.

Dewey Vick and Mrs. Norwood Lockett, my darling "Wild Plum,"[4] decorated the tables and, when Grace Mary was late because her plane was detained, Wild Plum stood with me to receive the guests.

After luncheon—with Grace Mary still absent—some of the guests spoke briefly and a few sang. Then came that awful sag that can ruin any party.

So I rose and said, "My dear friends of long standing, I am disposed, this afternoon, to confide one of my deepest secrets to you. In fairness to Wild Plum, whom some of you have met for the first time this afternoon, I should like to disclose that she is my illegitimate daughter."

There were audible gasps from my audience and from the stark expressions on their faces I understood that they were taking me a little too seriously, so I decided to make the story even more impossible.

"I had an affair with a sea captain with hypnotic blue eyes. I simply could not resist him. He was a Scandinavian with all of the fire and persuasiveness of his race. We travelled mainly in northern waters. We never married, of course, even after Wild Plum was born. I did not know nor care at the time that he had two wives before he met me and was divorced from neither of them. One lived in Trinidad and the other somewhere in Iceland.

"At length we were returning from Oslo in a small boat. My captain became so infuriated at the continual bawling of our child that he left me

---

4. According to her daughter Ann, Grace was a member of a group of eight women who met together regularly and who gave each other vegetal nicknames. Ruth Lockett was known as "Wild Plum." Ann thinks Grace was called "Thistle."

flat with my dear Wild Plum. I fed her on whale oil until she was old enough to eat the blubber and that accounts for her wonderful complexion and her beautiful figure."

Grace Mary had come into the room during my story and she was enchanted with the tale and with the effect it was producing. For, tall as the tale was, some of them believed it. In fact, I am sure that some few still do think it the truth, embellished to make confession easier.

Miss du Pont, one of our guests, was so charmed with it that she presented me with her necklace of costume jewels. A week later I had luncheon with Miss du Pont where she told me that the story did not sound as impossible as I thought. "But," she added, "how silly of anyone to think that, had it been true, you would have told it."

Father, you can be sure, also loved these occasional outbursts of mine, providing they were geared to the occasion. He admired complacency[5] in anyone, but he often remarked that complacency, if allowed to get out of hand, often breeds smugness. He abhorred smugness and would be quietly amused to see anyone who was bored or self-satisfied, jarred back to normalcy with a preposterous tale.

But never, never would he countenance a story that pointed up the shortcomings of anyone. In fact, I do not believe that he ever presumed to criticize the behavior of any person. Especially if that person was doing his best.

WHIPPING MATHER

One time, when Mather was quite young, he came home from school and tearfully reported that the teacher had taken a rubber hose to him.

I flew into a rage at the presumption of the teacher—daring to whip my child. I have said that I would do anything—even kill—in defense of my children, and I am sure that I mean it. I certainly was in a mood to do battle that day, but Father persuaded me to let him handle the matter. That was a mistake.

Instead of storming into the school and tearing the teacher to bits, he dispassionately got the other side of the story and came home full of com-

5. Perhaps she meant "contentment."

passion for the complexity of a teacher's problems of imparting knowledge and maintaining discipline with so many different temperaments to
deal with fairly.

I found out later, though not from Father, that Mather had been ridiculed by his playmates because he never had been whipped at school.
(And that was my fault because I had warned the teacher never to whip
my child.) But Mather had driven the teacher to desperate measures by
firing spit-balls at him to remove the stigma.

Chapter Fifteen

First and Second Marriages

Wise men contend that there is a reason and an explanation for every happening.

Why then, should I, who was so happily married to Father for so many years, rear three children who all were so unhappy in their first marriages? I confess that I have no reasonable answer.

To lay the blame on the prankishness of Fate seems trite, and an unjustifiable reward for all the good things he has released from his stores for me. But what other explanation is there?

First, Grace Mary wed Etienne de Pelissier de Bujac, of Albuquerque, New Mexico on the first day of January, in 1927.[1] Her husband, known to so many thousands as Bruce Cabot, of motion picture fame, seemed an ideal mate for my darling.[2]

Oakland was agog for a week before the ceremony and on New Year's day their entourage was escorted through Orlando behind a detail of motor police, while the fire bells and whistles welcomed them along their way. Theirs was the first marriage to be consummated[3] in the Episcopal Cathedral in Orlando.

Jennifer was born to them almost one year later.[4] Within another two years, they were divorced.

---

1. Etienne was 22 years old; Grace was only 17 years old.
2. Born 1904; died 1972. He started acting in 1931, when he no doubt changed his name, and starred in "King Kong" opposite Fay Wray in 1933.
3. She probably meant "performed."
4. On December 6, 1927.

On May 30th, 1930, Grace Mary and the illustrious James Allen Turner[5] of Columbia, Tennessee were wed. They are supremely happy in Highwood,[6] Illinois, with their two daughters, Jan Ann and Mary Beth; Jennifer[7] having married Russell P. Kelley, Jr. The Kelley's have made Palm Beach, Florida their home.

Next, Mather married Winifred Cagney on August 23, 1931 in Chicago. Winifred was the youngest daughter of James and Jennie Cagney, an old Chicago family. Their son Charles Frederic was born in Orlando and their daughter Mary Rozet was born in Chicago.

Mather now is married to Helen Mindlin of Los Angeles, California and they live most happily at Castle Hill, just a few miles from me.

Then, on September 20th, in 1934, my baby Ann married Richard Fletcher Baldwin, III, of Fall River, Massachussetts in the Episcopal church in Columbia, Tennessee, under omens which should have resulted in a lifetime of contentment for both. But that union also ended disastrously.

Ann now is the wife of John C. Fischbeck.[8] They live in Honolulu with their lovely youngsters, John III, Grace Harriette and Palmer Drexel.[9]

---

5. Born in Tennessee on November 15, 1902; died of a heart attack in Highwood, Illinois, on February 4, 1952, at 49 years of age.

6. Highwood is next to Highland Park.

7. Jennifer was adopted by James A. Turner, whom she called "Daddy."

8. Ann and John C. Fischbeck II were married in Oakland on November 29, 1937.

9. Born on June 3, 1940, in Honolulu; born on July 29, 1942, in Oakland, California (when her father was in the Navy and assigned to the Alameda Naval Air Station); born on February 12, 1944, in Chicago.

Chapter Sixteen

Hawaii

Of all of the places I have visited, Honolulu comes closest to being my favorite. When my health permits I expect to go there again to renew my acquaintances and perhaps to even the score with John, for he is at least two points ahead right now.

POINT ONE

When John[1] was courting Ann in Honolulu, they invited me one day to ride with them to the Wailea Country Club where, presumably, John had a business appointment.

I sat in the car for what seemed hours and hours, finally trying my patience to the point where I started the car and started for the hotel. At a crossroads a short distance from the club, I became confused and asked directions from a police officer. Soon it began to rain and I turned around to go back for my daughter.

This time the officer stopped me when I reached the crossroads.

"I thought you were headed for the Royal Hawaiian," said he.

I told him why I was returning but he was not satisfied.

"Sounds a little fishy to me. May I see your driving license?"

I had left my license at the hotel, not intending to drive, and I explained that fact to him. He was not at all impressed and showed quite plainly that

---

1. John Fischbeck was the general manager of the Royal Hawaiian Hotel on Waikiki when Grace, Fred and Ann were guests in the summer of 1937; he remained general manager until the attack on Pearl Harbor, when he joined the Navy. After the war he was once again general manager of the Royal Hawaiian from 1947 until 1957.

Figure 16.1.   Grace, Fred, their daughter Ann Fischbeck, and their granddaughter Jan Ann Turner

he did not believe me. He gave me a summons for traffic violation together with his personal opinions about Mainland tourists who came over to the Islands and expect to regulate laws to suit themselves.

We had quite an argument. I had come from the state which cherishes its tourist trade and I told him that Honolulu AND its police might do well to emulate us. But to no avail. Come to think about it, I never have known anyone who won an argument with a traffic policeman. I got the ticket with instructions to appear in traffic court at ten o'clock the next morning.

When I picked up Ann and John and told them of the incident, John said he was very sorry that I argued with the policeman, that the magistrates were quite strict about traffic violations, and that he doubted whether he could help me, but he would try.

Next morning I came downstairs early to go to court. Although Father advised me to pay the fine and forget it, I was looking forward to my appearance before the judge. I intended to amplify my remarks to the policeman with a lot more I had polished up during the night, and I told John so.

He went to the telephone and returned to say that he had succeeded in postponing the hearing until the next day at two o'clock.

Next morning he arranged another postponement for two days. This did not suit me at all. I was cooling off and I knew it, so I wanted to speak my piece without further delay. I insisted on going to court that morning.

When it could not be put off any longer, they told me that John had arranged the whole thing and that I had not been arrested at all.

POINT TWO

Another time John and Ann, Mr. and Mrs. Emery Todd, Mrs. Murphy and Mrs. McAlpin and I drove over to Tampa in two cars to see about some fruit.

In the Spanish Restaurant there John told Ann that he had met some man named Movario on the street. They were both quite excited about it, telling me that Movario was Oklahoma's most famous flying ace. John said that Mr. Movario was flying a private plane over to Havana that evening to pick up a party. The pilot had invited us to make the trip over with him, promising transportation for our return.

Most of our party refused to go but Hazella Todd and I decided to go anyway. Hazella was elated at this unexpected opportunity to get to Havana, if only for an hour or two.

Evening came and John started to take us to the airport. I protested that we were taking the wrong direction but John explained that he was heading for a private [air]port many miles from town.

We drove and drove until finally I recognized the street lights of Lakeland. Another hoax and he gloatingly was taking us home.

I wanted so badly to even things with him after that first episode. On their wedding day I intended to arrange for his arrest and overnight detention along their honeymoon route, but in the excitement of the day I forgot to make the final arrangements until too late.

I did express them a trunk full of old rags and shoes but I am afraid that fell a little flat.

BACK TO HONOLULU

You all know about Ann's illness and surgery that took us to Honolulu another time.[2]

John had been advising me that Ann was not up to par. Then he wrote that the doctor had decided Ann was a hypochondriac and not to worry too much about her condition.

One Sunday—John's father and mother were in Honolulu at the time— Ann hemmorhaged so badly she could not get out of bed. That was the day that most of the doctors were out of reach on the other side of the Island. The hospitals were crowded with emergency cases but they managed to get Ann into one of them for immediate surgery and multiple transfusions.

When John informed me that Ann had been given blood from Hawaiian donors I was horrified until my own doctor convinced me that I was most abysmally ignorant on that subject.

Ann's first words after the operation were a request to talk with me. They managed to rig a telephone to her bed and called us in Oakland. She wanted Father and me to come out at once. We both knew how gravely

2. According to Ann, in 1938 or 1939.

ill she was and we wanted to fly. But Father was then ill with the complications that were to take him from us, so flying was out of the question. In fact, the railroad company furnished a nurse to attend him across the country.

We were delayed getting to the west coast and then the steamship seemed to progress so slowly that I was frantic with anxiety. I could not eat or sleep.

Then one night I went up onto the sun deck because I could not bear the thought of bed. The beautiful indigo sky seemed close enough to touch. God was very near and I knew it.

"Dear God," I prayed, "I know you can see in my heart, my anxiety for Ann. Would it be contrary to your Plan of Things to give Your special blessing to John and my baby tonight?"

I looked at the stars and they were as bright as the lights on the ship below me. A sudden chill came over me and then an indescribable calm. I went to bed and was asleep almost at once. Nor was I anxious over Ann for the rest of the voyage. When we reached Honolulu I was not surprised to learn that she was recovering miraculously.

Later during that trip John took me to a cocktail party for a bride and groom. Father felt quite well that afternoon so he accompanied us. I wore a white chiffon overskirt with a red knit jacket which he particularly liked. Before the party was over, our friends said they wished to give a dinner for us at the country club that evening. We accepted but Father could not go.

John was to drive so I got Father to bed with some hot soup and went down to the lobby to meet John. There we both agreed that perhaps my skirt was a little too diaphanous, so I hurried back to our suite and slipped on a rather long pair of silk panties with elastic bottoms.

Almost as soon as we got under way I became so warm that I asked John to open the windshield. A moment later I was so chilly I had to draw my coat about me. During the ten minute drive this happened three times.

The groom wanted to dance at once and during that dance I had two more seizures. By then my arms and neck were so painful that I produced the excuse that I must hurry back to the hotel to make sure about Father's blankets.

In the taxi my teeth began to chatter, then I lost all muscular control. When we reached the hotel, the driver had to help me like a complete drunk, which he undoubtedly thought I was.

Father called John and between them they kept me from fainting with aromatic spirits until the ambulance arrived to take me to Queen's Hospital. There, three doctors decided that I had angina and administered emergency treatment for that. I was so miserable all that night.

Next morning, Ann came into my room very early, long before the nurses started their morning routine. I lay in bed with most of my body exposed, not caring about anything except relief. Then Ann noticed what none of the doctors had dreamed of looking for.

On the most intimate part of my body a scorpion[3] had fastened himself, and was poisoning me through my nervous system. He undoubtedly was in the little used garment I had hurriedly slipped into.

I was in hospital for three days and then they wanted to send a nurse home with me but I sent her back at once.

---

3. Perhaps a tick, which when magnified could be mistaken for some sort of scorpion.

Chapter Seventeen

Widowhood

Father's health did not improve. He was now content to wander among his favorite plants and trees with his pruning shears or to sit for hours under his pet virgin live oak tree where he now rests.

He never complained nor would he admit that he was experiencing any discomfort although his eyes often told a story of their own.

Toward the end of Father's long illness when his distress must have been most acute, he still insisted that everyone about him lead their normal lives. In fact, he was most annoyed if they did not. He was almost apologetic when he surmised that his ill-health might be a damper to their good spirits.

Figure 17.1. Charles Frederic Mather-Smith (1863-1941)

I will not set down here a recounting of my last days with Father.[1] Nor can I find the words to record my grief at that time, or to be rational in describing the horribly empty days and weeks that followed. If any of you remember my irresponsible

---

1. Charles Frederic Mather-Smith died on October 27, 1941, at age 77. Grace was 57 years old at the time.

behavior, my earnest hope is that you forget it forever. My thoughts now are not of the end, but of the beginning and the many happy, happy years in between.

I believe it to be true that the mind has capacity for but one consuming passion, be it grief or joy, constructive work or indolent scheming, love or hate. It is the passion that makes great statesmen and crafty dictators, miraculous healers or murderers. Or, more often, it makes normal beings from those who might otherwise go berserk.

With a tenacity I did not suspect I possessed, I managed to remove every thought from my mind except those things which needed doing. I worked from daylight until dark and then lay in bed and planned the duties for the next day until sleep came.

The jobs that Father had started or contemplated were the first order of business. Not with any sense of duty or gesture to his memory, but simply because Father was a constructive planner and the things he contemplated were those things which were best for Edgegrove Farms. Day after day, I drove myself and those about me with an energy that left no room for reflection or sorrow.

I know that I drove Robert Madison[2] almost to distraction. But somehow he understood what I was trying to do and he tried his best to please me.

My express fruit business started from scratch at that time. The introduction of the packing house, the extensive replantings in the gardens and groves and the shufflings of the furnishings in the house were all projects of that period. And interspersed were enforced holidays, usually spent travelling, when, instead of resting, I played as hard as I had been working.

I was so supremely happy that it had been possible for me to take over, more or less completely, the lives of two of my grandchildren—Mary Rozet and Charles Frederic. They furnished exactly the responsibility I needed: a family to raise and care for.

Mary Rozet was to be carefully educated while Frederic had to be given special thought. He, presumably, was the only chance to perpetuate the Mather-Smith name, so his future must be carefully considered.

I am sure that every mother has moments of comparatively lucid "hindsight." Tiny moments when she ponders whether, had she been able to

---

2. Grace's long-time chauffeur and faithful servant.

replace mother instinct with dispassionate objectiveness, her child might not have benefited in later life.

Now I was being given another chance, and the children would have all of the advantages of my experiences. They would be raised as models for all mothers to pattern their youngsters by.

But, of course, they were brought through their formative years exactly as all of you were. Instinct again prevailed. I can no more tell you of specific joys and moments of perplexity with them than I can recall similar instances with any of you, my darlings.

You can see that with all these activities, my entire plan was a success. Mentally, it was perfect. But I had forgotten the governing factor for its continuation. I neglected to guard my health.

THE RICE DIET

My blood pressure rose far above any safe measure, my heart became erratic and my nervous system was close to complete failure.

As you know, it was my heart that was most over-strained and I suffered an attack which the local doctors thought was the end for me. I was taken to hospital in Orlando where I remained in an oxygen tent before my specialist told Grace Mary that I could not live.

We had heard of the remarkable work of Doctor Kempner[3] at Duke Hospital in Durham, North Carolina and you children decided to take me there. My doctor had a high regard for Doctor Kempner—he had attended his lectures, as a matter of fact—and he was agreeable that I should make the trip, although he could not arrange to accompany me.

Part way by ambulance and then by train on a cot, with two nurses watching virtually every breath that I took, we finally landed at Duke. There they were so crowded that I could not have a room. For the first eight or nine hours I lay on a hard slab in the receiving ward while most of the doctors around the hospital came in and observed me from time to time. Obviously, some of them were curious why I was still living with a blood pressure of over three hundred. They seemed to take for granted the fact that I would not live long. Even Doctor Kempner was not optimistic.

3. In the 1930s and '40s, Dr. Walter Kempner treated patients with very high blood pressure, which was considered lethal and for which no other treatment was available anywhere, with what he called "the Rice Diet."

He mentioned my unusual case to a patient of his who was then recovering from a similar but not so aggravated a condition. That man was Mr. Harvey Smith, the president of the Smith Typewriter Company. Mr. Smith was so distressed that I might have to die on that hard slab that he arranged with the doctor to remove him to a hotel so that I might breathe my last in his comfortable bed.

But, as is so very obvious, I did not die. I responded to that wonderful doctor's treatment so promptly that I surprised him as much as the interns.

At first I was almost totally blind because of a recurrent kidney disorder. One eye was completely sightless and in the other I had only the dimmest vision. This condition also, the doctor cleared up permanently during my four months' stay there. The doctor's famous rice diet and total abstinence from water brought me back to health and have been my mainstays ever since.

UNDERTAKERS

I have laughed for years over jokes about ambulance-chasing lawyers, but I think the jokesters are missing something by not thinking up some good ones about temperature chart undertakers. Although I did not see the humor in my first visitors at Duke. During my second day there the first undertaker called. I was too ill to see him so he left his card and a two pound box of candy. After he broke the ice, so to speak, his competitors called with regularity. I could visualize them prowling the hall outside my door, each with a yardstick behind his back. When I was again able to take an interest in things, I sent for the mortician in Winter Garden, one of the few who had not tried to sell me a funeral while I was fighting to keep from having one, and arranged the final rites with him. For some time, I hope, still far, far away.

MORE SUITORS

During my life I have always tried to be tolerant toward the viewpoint of others. Nevertheless, my sense of propriety is sometimes strained with the effort of trying to justify the actions of another.

Father had been dead for less than five weeks when a close friend of his, a prominent Chicago clubman, called and, without too much pre-amble, proposed marriage. I was too shocked to consider it as an insult to Father.

Two weeks later another of his friends proposed that I marry him. I was outraged. I burst into tears which I could not stop. Grace Mary laughed at my emotion.

"Dad would consider that a compliment, Mother. He would say that they were men of discernment, that they appreciate you almost as much as he."

Later there was a doctor in Colorado Springs who wanted me to marry him. I was madly in love with him for about two weeks. Then one day he appeared in Florida suddenly. I was alone with Ann and John's children. They all had colds, were irritable, and at the moment of his visit devilishly possessive of me. He was tremendously annoyed. He said, quite undip-lomatically, that I was little more than a nursemaid—a servant—for my children. If I had any true love for him, it vanished without leaving a trace in that minute. I gave him back his ring—sapphires, not diamonds—and did not see him again.

Another earnest suitor was an oilman from Clinton, Oklahoma. He was one of the most interesting men I ever knew. He never had known his father and mother, both having died when he was an infant. He had been on his own since boyhood, with more struggle for existence in his back-ground than education. He was tall and rugged. A typical self-made man.

I never loved him madly but I admired him very much. He had edu-cated himself under tremendous difficulties. And a complete job he did of it, too. He owned an immense library and he was familiar with most of its contents. His special interest was the Far East. He knew the Orient so thoroughly that he was an expert on its geography, peoples, customs, laws and religions. Yet he never had been outside the United States.

He, on the other hand, adored me. Volubly, he idolized my appearance, my frankness and my devotion to family.

But when he caressed me I knew that I never could marry him, and told him so. He argued most persuasively until he knew that he could not hope to change my mind. Then he took my hand and placed a ring of three, four carat diamonds on my finger and said, "I wish to put this ring on your finger and I hope you will wear it and think of the one person who will always admire you in every way."

We corresponded regularly until I wrote him that I was about to marry Milo McAlpin. Then his letters to me ceased.

Chapter Eighteen

Last Thoughts

Considerably more than a year has gone to follow the growing procession into the past since I started writing these memoirs to you, my darlings. Many things have happened—most of them good, as usual. But a few have been less pleasant.

During the year I have been with each of you at one time or another. My choicest memories, you can be sure.

I have seen Jan Ann become a debutante with the loveliest parties within my recollection.[1] She reminds me so much of her mother when Grace Mary was her age. Also I have observed an increasing number of her mother's delightful qualities becoming evident in Mary Beth as she grows older.

I have watched Frederic graduate from Augusta Military Academy[2] with honors and listened to his enthusiastic reactions to his first European trip during the summer vacation. And I am happy that he now is enrolled at Virginia Military Institute for his higher education.

I am astonished at the completeness with which Mary Rozet has emerged from a charming adolescent to a very exciting young lady within a year.

Another highlight was the opportunity to watch over my Corky, Gay Gay and Tiger[3] for so short a time, and to thrill at the ecstasy with which they greeted their first sight of the beautiful fall leaves and their first snowstorm in Highwood.

---

1. On July 1, 1950, in Highland Park, Illinois.
2. In Fort Defiance, Augusta County, Virginia. It closed in 1984.
3. The nicknames of her daughter Ann's children.

And high among these memorabilia are my thoughts of my first and so far, my only great-grandbaby Russell III,[4] whom I have seen several times this year.

A not-so-pleasant record is that I have been ill another time this year. An amplified recurrence of my old malady. My recovery is slower—it has been over five months now—and since my hospitalization at Duke I know that it will never be a complete one. The damage to my heart has left scars which are permanent, irreparable.

My dear old clocks—I now have over thirty in the office and about the house—are forever reminding me that it is far, far later than it was when I started these pages.

My Swedish master's clock with its slow, measured beat, tells me with every tick that another second has been taken from the future and added to the past.

And to this I am resigned, but never resentful.

A year ago I was provoked that I could not conveniently make a pilgrimage to the Holy Land. Now I am happy that I did not go. Christ is not only in the Holy Land. He is here; He is everywhere. And the farther one tiptoes into the twilight, the nearer He comes. Here in Florida we are close to God. The sun, the moon and stars, the trees and flowers, all bespeak His nearness.

The prayer chair in my bedroom is well worn. But my communion with God is not at a set time. All day I offer Him thanks for all He has done for my family and me and to pray that Peace will soon come to this perplexed world.

---

4. Born on November 5, 1949, in West Palm Beach, Florida.

Epilogue

It was my plan, when I started these pages, to set down a significant number of episodes, together with a word or two of my philosophy, and to end them with a cheerful reference to my complete happiness here at Edgegrove Farms with my new husband, Milo McAlpin. All satisfactory stories should end in that fashion.

You will recall that I pondered over possible reasons for each of you experiencing an unfortunate marriage. Fate, I contemplated, should not be blamed. Now I am not so sure.

I am sure all of you were relieved when I married Milo—a family friend and admirer for so many years.[1] My loneliness would be at an end and I now should have someone to love and protect me. But we were incompatible from the beginning.

My doctors tell me that a major contributing cause of my recent heart involvement was the accumulated result of my complete effort to overcome a situation which could not improve for lack of cooperation.

Some of you know that Milo and I have separated within the past month and that my divorce will be granted early in August.

And with that, my darlings, my life's story is not only complete, but it is projected some eight weeks into the future.[2]

---

1. Grace and Milo married at Edgegrove Farms in April 1949. Milo was 74 years old, and it was his first marriage. In June and July, they spent their honeymoon in Honolulu at the Royal Hawaiian Hotel, where John Fischbeck was once again general manager and Ann's and his family lived. As unconventional as ever, Grace invited her 17-year-old granddaughter Jan Ann Turner to accompany Milo and her on her honeymoon, a memory that Jan Ann cherishes.
2. So this memoir closes in June 1951.

Figure E.1.   Grace with her eight grandchildren at Blowing Rock, North Carolina, in 1946

Afterword By The Editor

In August 1951, Grace and Milo McAlpin divorced after two years of marriage. Shortly thereafter, Grace moved into the caretaker's cottage at Edgegrove Farms, where she was looked after by her faithful servant Robert Madison, whom she affectionately called Madison.

On February 25, 1952, the entire contents of the main house at Edgegrove Farms were sold at auction at Trosby Galleries in Palm Beach.

When her health declined and she could no longer live independently, Grace moved into a room at the West Orange Memorial Hospital in Winter Garden, which she had helped to build; the chief doctor said that Miss Grace could stay as long as she liked, free of charge. At that time Milo was living in the Edgewater Hotel in Winter Garden; he visited Grace every day.

Grace died on January 1, 1962. Her casket was first placed in the family mausoleum at Edgegrove Farms, alongside that of her first husband, Charles Frederic Mather Smith. After the mausoleum was vandalized, their caskets were moved to the Oakland cemetery, where they lie next to each other today.

In 1963, the house at Edgegrove Farms was demolished and the property was sold to developers.

OAKLAND TODAY

Much has changed since Grace and Fred built Edgegrove Farms. After Fred died in 1941, Lake Apopka, until then a fisherman's paradise, became polluted by effluents discharged by the farms along its shores, killing the fish and closing the fish camps. Thanks largely to the efforts of the Friends of Lake Apopka (FOLA), restoration of the lake started in 1991; it is still underway.

Citrus had long been West Orange County's leading economic activity, but freezing temperatures in the 1980s devastated orange trees. Citrus production fell abruptly and has never recovered.

Oakland (population around 3,000) is today a sleepy suburb of its much larger neighbor Winter Garden (population around 42,000). Indeed, Oakland's town lines have been redrawn, so that the property on which the West Orange Country Club once stood is now in Winter Garden. What remains, however, is a rare corner of Old Florida, with clapboard houses still lining quiet streets bordered by majestic white oak trees dripping with Spanish moss.

Downtown Oakland now consists of a post office, a bank and a town office. The hotel, grocery store and opera house are long gone. The town park where Grace used to invite all the town's children to celebrate Grace Mary's birthdays, now named Speer Park after Oakland's founder and leading promoter Judge James Gamble Speer, and a smaller version of Grace Park, are still there. So is the Oakland cemetery, where Grace and Fred and Milo are buried, along with many of their friends. Edgegrove Farms is now the Southern Oaks subdivision, where single-family houses on tidy lots overlook the lake. The original gates marking the main entrance to Edgegrove Farms can still be seen on Tubb Street, alongside a house near the new entrance to the subdivision.

Perhaps the biggest change is the removal of the Orange Belt railroad tracks. In their place is the paved West Orange Trail, which runs for 22 miles on the right of way of the old tracks from Apopka, through downtown Winter Garden, to Oakland. Renting bikes in downtown Winter Garden, which has been beautifully restored, and following the West Orange Trail west, past Lakeville High School in Tildenville and then on to Grace Park, is the perfect way to visit Oakland.[1] While in Winter Garden, drop by the Winter Garden Heritage Foundation and see the section of the museum dedicated to "Miss Grace," the *grande dame* of Oakland.

---

1. In fact, the first four miles of the West Orange Trail were inaugurated at Grace Park on September 3, 1994.

THE MATHER-SMITH FAMILY TODAY

Grace is survived today by one child, five grandchildren, 12 great-grandchildren, 26 great-great-grandchildren, and four great-great-great-grandchildren (so far).

Grace's "baby" Ann (known to all as "Moosie") celebrated her 104th birthday this year. Ann adored her mother. When she celebrated her 90th birthday in 2004, she asked guests to "come as your secret desire." Her guests came as kings and queens, tennis champions, pirates, big game hunters—even angels. Annie came dressed as her mother. This book is dedicated to her.

Appendix

MATHER-SMITH FAMILY

The Mather-Smith family traces its roots back to England, France and Germany, and includes some distinguished forebears and cousins.

Henry Smith and his brothers James and Ichabod immigrated to Massachusetts from England around 1630, only 10 years after the Pilgrims landed at Plymouth Rock on the Mayflower. The Smith family motto was "Carpe Diem" (Seize the Day).

In 1720, Henry's great-grandson Samuel married Jerusha Mather, daughter of Reverend Cotton Mather, the influential Puritan minister of Boston's Old North Church, who was instrumental in securing convictions in the Salem witch trials in 1692. (His father, Increase Mather, and grandfather, Richard Mather, were also "divines.") Samuel and Jerusha had four children. The eldest, Dan, married Keziah DeVotion (later spelled Devotion) in 1752; her father, Rev. Ebenezer DeVotion, had come to America from France. (Dan's younger brother Cotton Mather Smith, a long-serving minister in Sharon, Connecticut, married Temperance Worthing; their son John Cotton Smith was Governor of Connecticut from 1812 to 1817.) According to family lore, the mother of Keziah, Naomi Taylor, was descended from King Egbert (802-839), the first Saxon king recognized as sovereign of all England.[1]

Dan and Keziah's great-grandson John Smith married Lucy Laney Bradner in 1813. Their son George Cotton Smith founded, together with his cousin Josiah H. Bradner and William G. Warren, what became Brad-

---

1. Richard S. Bull, Jr. (Fred's grandson) characterized this claim as "sheer balderdash."

ner Smith & Company, a paper company, in Chicago in 1852. William Warren soon left the firm and Josiah Bradner died in 1857. George's brother John Bradner Smith moved from New York State to Chicago to join the firm in 1858; his brother Charles Mather Smith moved to Chicago in 1858, probably from Ogdensburg, New York, and joined the company in 1871; he became President in 1879.

Charles Mather Smith (born September 27, 1831; died June 16, 1912) married Sarah Emily (or Emilie) Rozet (born January 28, 1839; died March 26, 1903) on October 3, 1860. Their three children were all born in Chicago: Francis Anthony Drexel, Mary Rozet (life-long supporter of Hull House and devoted friend of its founder Jane Addams), and Charles Frederic Mather Smith (who, according to his daughter Ann, started to hyphenate his name in the 1900s so that he would no longer receive mail intended for his neighbor in Highland Park, Illinois, J.P. Smith). Charles Frederic (known as "C.F." or "Fred") worked in the family business his entire life. He served as President of Bradner Smith & Company from his father's death in 1912 until 1929, when he was succeeded by his son-in-law Richard S. Bull (the husband of his daughter from his first marriage); he then served as Chairman of the Board of Directors until his death in 1941.

Fred's mother Sarah Rozet Smith was descended from two continental European immigrant families. George Hollenback and his wife Maria Catherina emigrated from Wuertenburg, Germany, to Pennsylvania in 1717. Their grandson Col. Matthias Hollenbeck (born 1752; died in Wilkes Barre, Pennsylvania, in 1829) fought in the Revolutionary War. His daughter Sarah married Jean Jacques Roset (born in Lyons, France, in July 1764; died in Germantown, Pennsylvania, on January 26, 1850), who had fled from France to Vienna with his brother Nicholas and their Austrian mother during the French Revolution (their father Jean Marie Roset had died in 1781), and then emigrated to Philadelphia in 1792 and changed his name to Jacob Rozet. Their son John Rozet (born September 3, 1794; died in Philadelphia on October 9, 1870) and his wife Mary Ann Laning (born in Wyoming Valley, Pennsylvania, on February 28, 1807; died in Owego, New York, in March 1834) were the parents of five children; the last was Sarah Emily (or Emilie), who was called "Sallie" (born January 28, 1836; died March 26, 1903).

Sarah's older sister Ellen Bicking Rozet (born September 18, 1830; died in Philadelphia in November 1891) married Anthony Joseph Drexel on August 13, 1850. Her father-in-law Francis Martin Drexel came to Philadelphia from Dornbirn, Austria, in 1817, and in 1836 founded the banking house Drexel & Company, which would later become Drexel Burnham & Lambert. His son Anthony Joseph became a member of Drexel & Company in 1847. In 1871, he founded the merchant bank Drexel, Morgan & Co. with his partner John Pierpont Morgan; upon Drexel's death in 1893, the name of the bank was changed to J.P. Morgan & Co. Sarah was close to her sister Ellen, and she named her second son Francis Anthony Drexel Smith; her granddaughter Ann Mather-Smith Fischbeck carried on the tradition when she named her younger son Palmer Drexel Fischbeck.

About The Editor

As Grace noted in her memoir, Russell III was her first "great-grandbaby," soon to be followed by eleven others. His grandmother Grace Mary married the future Bruce Cabot (of King Kong fame) when she was only 17 years old, and their daughter Jennifer was born a year later. As recounted in her grandmother's memoir, Jennifer married Russell P. Kelley, Jr. of Lake Bluff, Illinois, in 1946. They moved to Palm Beach, Florida, in 1949, where the editor was born and raised. His great-grandmother Grace made several trips to Palm Beach to visit the Kelley family, as well as her widowed daughter Grace Mary Turner and granddaughter Mary Beth, and the editor and his mother once visited Grace at Edgegrove Farms towards the end of her long and eventful life.

After a career as an international business lawyer which took him around the world, Russell Kelley returned to live in Palm Beach in 2012, where he and his wife (who was born in Orlando) have enjoyed rediscovering Florida. Another discovery was the memoir written by his great-grandmother, which proved the point so eloquently made by Grace in her introduction: Without the memoir, he would have remembered Grace as an old lady sitting in the shadows of a dark house surrounded by large oak trees dripping with Spanish moss. He is grateful that, thanks to her memoir, he now has a vivid sense—to use Grace's words—of the substance of her life: her fortunes, her reverses, her joys, her sorrows and her loves. It is a wonderful gift to receive from an earlier generation.